Explorations in Legal Geography

Addressing the issue of scale in governance, legal and extra-legal, the book draws on post-colonial studies, Indigenous geography and empirical and historical studies of the legal logics of Empire.

This book examines legal frameworks across six descending scales. Beginning with a global perspective centred on Global South viewpoints and globalisation critiques, it then explores imperial legal structures. Next, it addresses the nation-state scale, predominant in both mainstream and critical legal scholarship, with particular focus on challenging notions of ethnic homogeneity. The examination continues at the local level, analysing how various governing bodies exercise authority within their jurisdictions. It then narrows to consider 'home' as both a physical and legal construct, revealing how property concepts intertwine with social relationships. Finally, it investigates the human body as a governance site through queer legal studies, queer geography, and feminist scholarship that documents how female bodies specifically have become objects of legal and extra-legal control. Concluding by considering the regulatory dilemmas that have plagued authorities as they navigate the various scales of governance considered here.

Explorations in Legal Geography will be of considerable interest to students and scholars of legal geography, socio-legal studies, and criminology.

Mariana Valverde is professor emeritus at the Centre for Criminology and Sociolegal Studies, University of Toronto.

Explorations in Legal Geography

Law, Space and Regulation

Mariana Valverde

Routledge
Taylor & Francis Group
a GlassHouse Book

First published 2026
by Routledge
4 Park Square, Milton Park, Abingdon, Oxon OX14 4RN

and by Routledge
605 Third Avenue, New York, NY 10158

a GlassHouse book

Routledge is an imprint of the Taylor & Francis Group, an informa business

British Library Cataloguing-in-Publication Data
A catalogue record for this book is available from the British Library

Library of Congress Cataloging-in-Publication Data
Names: Valverde, Mariana, 1955- author
Title: Explorations in legal geography: law, space and regulation / by Mariana Valverde.
Description: Abingdon, Oxon [UK]; New York, NY: Routledge, 2026. | Includes bibliographical references and index.
Identifiers: LCCN 2025032781 (print) | LCCN 2025032782 (ebook) | ISBN 9781041009832 hardback | ISBN 9781041009818 paperback | ISBN 9781003612551 ebook
Subjects: LCSH: Law and geography | Law and geography--Political aspects | Sociological jurisprudence | Criminology
Classification: LCC K487.G45 V35 2026 (print) | LCC K487.G45 (ebook) | DDC 340--dc23/eng/20250728
LC record available at https://lccn.loc.gov/2025032781
LC ebook record available at https://lccn.loc.gov/2025032782

ISBN: 978-1-041-00983-2 (hbk)
ISBN: 978-1-041-00981-8 (pbk)
ISBN: 978-1-003-61255-1 (ebk)

DOI: 10.4324/9781003612551

Typeset in Times New Roman
by Deanta Global Publishing Services, Chennai, India

Contents

Introduction

This book is an introduction to the field of legal geography. It is meant as a primer that can be used as a course text, in law courses as well as in geography courses, including urban geography, and also in related fields such as urban anthropology, legal anthropology and urban planning. Urban planning instructors influenced by the rise of postcolonial studies will find this text more appropriate than most existing textbooks.

The field of legal geography has emerged from two sides, as is often the case with socio-legal studies. It emerged first among legal studies scholars and criminologists who were paying close attention to the ways in which governments, local governments in particular, deprived since the 1970s (mainly by appeal courts) of the capacious social-control Victorian-era category of 'vagrancy', turned to regulating the same types of people (the 'usual suspects') and similar problems (namely disruptions of the hegemonic social and legal order) through a variety of spatial means.

Examples of these efforts to govern disorderly urban denizens without breaching human rights statutes include non-legal measures, such as the 'bumproof' park benches designed to prevent sleeping that now grace urban parks in numerous countries. Another, more legal example consists of by-laws targeting certain times and spaces. These new-ish by-laws made certain things illegal on a site-specific basis, activities that are otherwise legal (say, prohibiting drinking alcohol in certain public spaces, not by means of general Prohibition laws but targeting only certain spaces, with drinking in one's own home or in a public restaurant remaining legal).

The phrase atrributed to French intellectual Andre Breton to the effect of 'the law in its majesty forbids the rich as well as the poor to sleep under bridges' is well known. Indeed, it could act as epigraph for the whole of this book. The phrase attributed to Breton points to the phenomenon of governing the underclasses through spatial means while formally complying with equal rights and civil rights laws.

Relatively new spatially oriented rules can and do coexist with a formal legal culture of equal rights and 'the rule of law', a legal culture which developed primarily in the 1960s and 1970s.

DOI: 10.4324/9781003612551-1

In some countries, notably Britain, there are no written constitutional rights because there is no written constitution. However, since the UK was for a long time a member of the European Union, after the Brexit process initiated in 2016, some national statutes attempted to preserve for people in Britain the rights that they had gained through the EU. The situation in Britain is thus unusual internationally; almost every other advanced capitalist country has a written constitution that ensures formal legal equality and some degree of personal protection from state overreach.

However, the material in this book applies to Britain as well. Whether there is a written constitution guaranteeing certain rights or not, rich people might well be subject to the same formal law as the poor, as the phrase attributed to Breton puts it: but wealthier people have little if any need to find shelter outdoors, and hence what looks like a 'rule of law' rule, treating people equally in a formal sense, has very different real-life results for each group. As legal scholar Jeremy Waldron put it in one of the first analyses of the legal situation of urban homeless people, we all need a place in which to carry out everyday tasks such as eating, sleeping, defecating, showering and so on. The need for a space in which to carry out daily activities is something that we all experience: but only unhoused individuals are forced to carry out these activities in the public realm.

Prohibitions on using public spaces to carry out these necessary activities are particularly hard, therefore, on those who also lack access to the private spaces of homes, restaurants, gyms, etc.[1] Indeed, one could say that legal geography studies, among other things, how legal tools targeting spaces and times require drawing a sharp line between 'public' and 'private'. The very division of public vs private is at one level the result of law. Private spaces are granted, generally, much more by way of rights protection than spaces deemed public. The Canadian courts that pondered for many years whether a private car should be treated by police as private, or as public if parked in a legal parking space downtown, or travelling on the street, are not unusual internationally. Rules about drinking and about sexual commerce almost everywhere draw or assume a sharp line between public and private, even if the specific content of those two categories shifts over time, or from place to place, as courts decide such questions as to whether the garbage bins left out on the sidewalk are 'public' and thus open to police inspection without any need for a warrant.

In general those of us who do have access to either residential or commercial spaces in which to carry out everyday activities do not suffer the same consequences from the prohibitions that target public spaces. And the population that enjoys both access to private homes and access to commercial spaces

1 Jeremy Waldron, 'Homelessness and Community' *University of Toronto Law Journal* vol. 50 no. 4 (2000) 371–406.

is generally already privileged, by contrast with the population that has no spaces but public ones in which to live and carry on everyday activities. Rules that target behaviours regarded as problematic (e.g. eating while riding public transit, drinking beer or liquor in public parks) have a highly differential impact on different demographics.

Hence the majesty of the law, which in liberal regimes is meant to to apply to everyone equally, can be made compatible with law enforcement practices that are by no means equally distributed amongst the population. Formally we are all equal – equal before the law, often seen as a key element of 'the rule of law' – but in reality some are more targeted than others. The privileged citizens who have pleasant private spaces in which to live their lives by reason of their income (including coffee shops and high-end restaurants and gyms, not just homes) are freer than others, in reality.

Now on to the second point of this introduction. Legal scholars, especially those affiliated with 'law and society' or (what is the same but goes by different names outside of the United States) socio-legal studies, including legal anthropology and legal sociology, often highlight legal issues and conflicts around *jurisdiction*.

These include the classic jurisdictional questions of who is the sovereign of or over a particular space (territorial jurisdiction), or who has what powers (functional jurisdiction, an example being whether a situation falls under family law or the criminal law). Those two conventional forms of jurisdiction (territorial and functional) often give rise to questions that are mainly posed in binary, either-or fashion: either this peak of the Pyrenees is in France or it is in Spain, or this issue is within the jurisdiction of a family court, not a criminal court. But the world is not so simple as to be amenable to binary distinctions.

A good example of jurisdictional complications is the very first scene of the much-watched TV drama 'The Bridge'. As the show begins, a corpse is found on the bridge that unites but also separates Sweden and Denmark. It is at first unclear which police force has jurisdiction. Much of the plot thus depends on the question of jurisdiction – and police actors might be interested in abdicating jurisdiction (so that the corpse becomes another force's problem) more than in claiming jurisdiction. Either way (whether abdicating or claiming), the binary questions about whether sovereign A or B has jurisdiction do not capture questions that one could call 'qualitative' or 'sociological'.

What I here call the qualitative dimension of governance is not always a deliberate choice on the part of authorities. There are jurisdictional divides that somehow seem normal and even natural, usually for the sole reason that they have a long history. For example it somehow makes sense to politicians as well as citizens that trash collection is almost everywhere regarded as municipal.

The fact that the numerous climate disasters of recent years might suggest that higher levels of government ought to take some responsibility for pollution, as well as for recycling and garbage disposal, does not change people's habits in regard to expectations about which jurisdiction is responsible for what problems. People somehow know that if the trash is not collected that is the fault of the municipality.

One of the tasks of legal geography is to provide tools with which ordinary people can pose questions about the right 'scale' to govern a particular problem. It could well be, for example, that the current environmental crisis might lead to a reconsideration of jurisdiction in matters of pollution, recycling, and managing 'natural' disasters such as floods and hurricanes.

Whilw trash disposal is seen as 'naturally' municipal, for almost every politician, international migration is assumed to be everywhere a responsibility of the central state. Passengers arriving in foreign airports usually encounter 'national police' when offering their passports to official scrutiny. This is an act that takes jurisdiction for granted, as if the scale of the police force scanning our passports were immovable or dictated by God himself. Local police officers may play some role in airports, often as nothing but glorified security guards; but local police are not usually seen as the 'right' body to police borders.

In the United States, the question of scale and the related question of jurisdiction has been complicated by the fact that ICE immigration enforcement officers wear jackets that say 'POLICE' on their backs. That is the case although strictly speaking they are not police but federal agents.[2] The United States has an interesting history of legal jurisdiction in law enforcement because for many decades, perhaps centuries, the federal government was not supposed to have any law enforcement powers. Creating the FBI required a huge amount of expenditure of political capital. And with the fall of the Soviet Union and the supposed end of the Cold War, it was not a foregone conclusion that the FBI, long concerned with threats to national security, would survive. Fortunately the mythical image of the 'serial killer' was invented just in time to rescue the FBI's budget.[3]

2 Not all the people sporting 'police' jackets are actually police, in the sense of holding the special, extensive powers granted by law to police officers. In my own university, campus security officers used to sport the word 'police' on their uniforms and their vehicles, for many years. Eventually they were forced to change their designation to what they really are, which is 'special constables'. Special constables, in Ontario at least, do not have the power to arrest or detain people, and they do not wear regularly wear guns. Hence they are more akin to private security guards than to public police, although they are still within the public sector.

3 The invention of the 'serial killer' is variously attributed to two FBI agents, one of them agent John Douglas, famously fictionalized in the Hollywood movie *Silence of the Lambs*. The film also popularized and glamourized the 'Behavioural Analysis Unit', a forensic entity within the FBI thought to be the main site of expertise in 'serial' killers. In the United States, local police forces have jurisdction over all murders, but it became a habit to call in the FBI if a 'serial killer' was being sought. British readers might ponder the fact that Jack the Ripper was not called a serial killer, at the time of his murders or afterwards. Similarly, some of Agatha Christie's murderers kill more than once, but her work predates the 'serial killer' category.

But the main point here is that assumptions about jurisdiction are embedded in our everyday lives. Jurisdiction as it has developed in a particular region of the world or in a specific country is usually taken for granted. Most urban and even suburban residents somehow know that trash issues are legally municipal, and are ready to call their city councillor or city staff when wanting to denounce someone for illegal trash disposal.

If an oil spill wrecks a beach on the sea or ocean that is regularly used for bathing, however, the local municipality is not usually expected to be the sole responder. Debates about whether the oil company or the national state should pay for the clean-up can and often do arise, and are often settled by courts asked to divide up jurisdiction: but the local municipality is not generally expected to handle a major sea-based or river-based oil spill on its own.

Often, in this type of complicated situation it is insurance companies, not state actors, that settle among themselves the question of jurisdiction, usually via the concomitant question of financial responsibility. This raises the spectre of 'private' jurisdiction – which in law includes coercive corporate rules such as dress codes, or in a university context, student discipline rules such as those governing cheating. Some jurisdictions, therefore, are private – for instance, the myriad rules issued by condominium boards. As seen in the condo example, private jurisdiction can enforce micromanagement-style rules that no public governmental body could issue. That is one of the most interesting aspects of what I have been calling in other work 'the game of jurisdiction'. For example, condominium boards can dictate the colour of blinds that are visible from the outside of the building, which no municipality in most countries could legally do. Such boards of owners can even dictate the maximum weight of allowable pets.

This is what one could call 'everyday jurisdiction' – the assumptions embedded in everyday life and in local culture about who is responsible for what and where, and who is authorized to issue what type of rule. Sometimes ordinary citizens purposively confuse the issue by using the vague term 'they' – as in, 'they haven't got public transit properly organized in this city'.

The vague term 'they', a powerful enabler of populism that builds on the implicit binary of 'we' (the people) vs. 'they' (authorities) lacks legal specifity. Inquiries into jurisdiction are therefore necessary in many practical situations.

In fact there is no 'they' that is responsible for, say, excessive condo construction blocking vehicular traffic in the inner city. Some knowledge of constitutional law and administrative law is thus very useful when attempting to move citizen discontent beyond the populist blaming of 'they' and toward a more concrete analysis of who is supposed to do what. Paying attention to the details of jurisdiction tends to eliminate the vagueness of the populist 'they', which is one of the benefits of taking jurisdiction seriously and critically.

The study of jurisdiction, long neglected by critical legal scholars, or dismissed, especially by critical legal scholars, as merely technical,[4] draws our attentionto the more interesting question, from a social science point of view, of whether particular scales of governance are qualitatively unique. That in my view is the central question of legal geography. And that is the reason why this book is structured by what geographers call 'scale', which overlaps a great deal with what lawyers call 'jurisdiction', although the two terms are not coterminous.

The question of whether particular scales of governance have distinct features has been most overtly tackled by urban studies, urban planning and in legal studies of city governance. It is within urban studies broadly understoood that critical questions about the relationship between styles of governance and scale or jurisdiction have been posed most explicitly.

This brings us to the third and final section of the introduction – centering on the meaning and significance of 'scale', in its relation to legal jurisdiction. One such question about the qualitative aspect of jurisdiction is: 'do cities have certain characteristic ways of posing and answering governance questions?' The urban-studies focus on 'seeing like a city'[5] is best understood in contrast to to the far more heavily studied governing gaze of 'the state'.

Although the two modes of governing, and the two jurisdictions, are often intertwined in practice (including through funding arrangements that divide financial responsibility among levels of government, arrangements that are especially common in federal or multinational countries). 'The state' is not a large city, and the city is not a small state.[6] There are significant qualitative differences between scales of governance that are not captured by conventional diagrams featuring quantities of territory or space. The EU, for example, is not just bigger than France or Germany. It has certain functional jurisdictions that individual states lack.

The crucial question of whether particular scales of governance, and particular legal regimes, are qualitatively distinct has often been asked by historians of legal and state governance as well as theoretically inclined legal studies scholars and urban geographers.

4 See Mariana Valverde, *Chronotopes of Law: Scale, Jurisdiction, and Governance* (London, Routledge, 2019).

5 Ash Amin and Nigel Thrift, *Seeing Like a City* (London, Polity Press, 2017) and Mariana Valverde, 'Seeing Like a City: The Dialectic of Modern and Premodern Knowledges in Urban Governance' *Law and Society Review* 45, 2 (2011), 277–313.

6 Of course there are some contemporary city-states, perhaps most notably Singapore, and Hong Kong until recently. Historically there were many cities that were also republics, such as Venice, Florence, and other Italian mini-republics, but by and large these gave way to nation-states, as was the case with Italy, which only came into existence as a nation-state in the late nineteenth century, along with Germany.

To reiterate: 'seeing like a city' has historically been rather different, qualitatively, from the better known logic that James Scott influentially dubbed 'seeing like a state'.[7] That is a claim about both jurisdiction and the quality of governance that has received much attention in the last decade or two. While individual scholars focus on different features and different legal techniques, it has been shown in numerous studies, historical as well as contemporary, that *pragmatic* approaches to managing concrete problems and risks – best exemplified, in the common law, by the law of nuisance, which is always, by definition, site-specific, and which requires not only a specified act but some real person who is bothered by it, since without bother or harm there is no nuisance – have characterized urban governance since medieval times.

The more abstract and more rationalistic or merely rational spatial logic of 'seeing like a state', not coincidentally more likely than local governance to be number-driven and based on expert knowledges, stands in contrast to the rather pragmatic and even low-brow logic that has been identified by its particular scale – 'seeing like a city'.

Seeing like a state would cover a range of projects, not all initiated by a modern nation-state: projects such as the Egyptian Pyramids, the Roman Empire's sewers, and the giant hydroelectric dams that have been built across Asian rivers for several decades now. It also applies to the 'New Deal' that president Franklin D Roosevelt put in place as a remedy for the Great Depression, which relied on massive infrastructure projects to employ the unemployed.

'Seeing like a city' applies to the pragmatic logic of the 'fence viewers', the first city bureaucrats I sought to observe at work. Fence viewers (an old British colonial term first used to indicate minor officials who literally marked off the fences separating farms from each other) are employed today in the Toronto city bureaucracy. They literally go to people's backyards to mediate intra-neighbour disputes about fences. In doing their work, the fence viewers (as recounted to me by a different city official) don't pay much attention to established numbers, such as the maximum height of backyard fences. Instead they provide on-site mediation, taking into account the particular social relations that make one neighbour complain to city hall about another. A mediated solution is just fine for them and for their bosses, even if the resulting fence is not in formal compliance with the fence by-law.

Of course not all human settlements are cities. Part of the problem inherited by legal geography from the large literature on urban studies is the question of whether rural and suburban municipalities can or do in fact share the 'seeing like a city' logic. Often, 'cities' are the intended policy audience of research articles and reports. Small municipalities rarely have specialized

7 James Scott, *Seeing Like A State: How Cetain Schemes to Improve Humankind Have Failed* (New Haven CT, Yale University Press, 1999).

departments and a host of experts on their payroll, or experts who can be hired as consultants to supplement municipal employees. Small municipalities tend to be followers rather than leaders in what is now called 'innovation' – innovation being a term that suggests public-private collaboration and also a micro-local scale. (This is not necessary: the New Deal was certainly an innovative enterprise at a large scale. But today innovation is largely thought of in terms of pilot projects and experimental forms: the New Deal logic has become old-fashioned and lacking in both 'innovation' and 'entrepreneurship', qualities that are associated with the private sector but seep into governmental decisions.)

There is a certain amount of governing space or governing 'daylight' that separates 'the city' from 'the municipality'. This is especially the case in places such as the United States, where incorporated municipalities are often far smaller in area and much more numerous than the socioeconomic conglomerates that the word 'cities' calls to mind. Los Angeles, for example, appears to many as a city, and it is often said to be the second largest in the United States after New York. Los Angeles County, however, includes 88 incorporated municipalities (such as Hollywood and West Hollywood) as well as some unincorporated areas. People living in Beverly Hills or West Hollywood might say that they live in LA but not quite. That is accurate, in that the property taxes paid by the wealthy people in those highly select expensive municipalities for rich people cannot be easily or automatically routed to poorer, largely Hispanic and Black areas, as would happen if regional integration and amalgamation were realities. Hence the importance of the scale of municipal incorporation, which otherwise sounds like the most boring legal topic ever.

This initial discussion of the differences between 'seeing like a city' and 'seeing like a state' is presented here as an example of how a legal geography lens can help in the understanding of how different entities, with different powers, not only govern their assigned *space* but also govern a variety of people and problems *through space*. *Space* is of course the central category for geographic studies in general.

The shift from governing persons directly through their status or identity to governing people and problems indirectly through space and through spatial measures hence requires some understanding, on the part of legal actors, of the spatial dynamics that have long formed the 'meat and potatoes' of the geographic enterprise.

An example from a highly 'practical' area of law may help to illustrate this point.

Planning lawyers, especially those working for municipalities, ritually intone that planning law and policy does not govern or even see people, individually or in groups. That is technically true. If a town has a by-law that prohibits sleeping under town bridges, or sleeping/camping in public parks, that by-law is neutral as to persons, and does not formally discriminate. A rich person who happens to sleep under a bridge would in theory be as liable to being fined as a poor homeless person – even though we all know that the actual probability of a rich person being found sleeping under a bridge is very low to nonexistent.

Old-time vagrancy statutes made it illegal to have the *status* of 'vagrant', 'beggar' or (a Canadian legal curiosity) a 'nightwalker', defined as a female who is out at night in public spaces without a good excuse. More recent laws and by-laws (ordinances, in the United States) that are designed to uphold urban order also tend to govern the usual suspects, but do so *through space* rather than identity or status. Municipalities generally have the power to issue 'place, time and manner' rules governing the uses to which public space can be put. In practice, time and space conditions often pile up or are thought of as going together. Of course that affects some groups more than others (as the now bulging literature on Black and especially African-American experiences with place, space and power suggest).[8]

Temporal limits are often added to space-specific rules, or used instead of spatial measures. Many municipalities ban camping in public parks, for example, but only at nighttime. Conversely, in some jurisdictions municipalities are not allowed to treat homelessness as illegal unless there is no space available in municipal shelters for homeless people.[9]

Chapter Organization

Chapter 1 is devoted to the scale associated with colonialism and imperialism. Much of the critical work on imperial governance has been carried out by historians, but such work should be of interest to legal geography, especially since at present it is unclear whether we are merely dealing with the present-day consequences of various kinds of colonialism or whether we are witnessing the rise of a 'new imperialism', in David Harvey's words. Seeking to avoid

8 The subfield known as 'Black' geography is largely dominated by African-American writers and sources (as is 'critical race theory', the equivalent within legal studies). In the global South, scholars of many activities including urban planning often talk about 'racial capitalism' as the main mode of production, not just capitalism in general. Katherine McKrittick, often cited as the inventor of Black geography due to the success of her 2006 book *Demonic Grounds*, utilizes some non-American writers, notably Dionne Brand and Marlene Nourbese Philip (both Canadian poets of Afro-Caribbean origin). Black scholars who are not in the United States have produced work that is highly relevant to questions of space and time, but the participation of African scholars or people of African descent not in the United States in the global academic literature is still very much a minority pursuit.

9 In the United States, the leading case on this features the tiny city of Grants Pass, Oregon. An even-handed treatment of the problem of homelessness from the point of view of municipal and state officials is presented in the *amicus curiae* brief by California governor Gavin Newsom submitted to the court in that case (available freely online at https://www.supremecourt.gov/DocketPDF/23/23-175/302201/20240304155924650_Newsome%20Amicus%20Brief%203-4-2024.pdf

crystal-ball exercises of predicting the future, I do not in this chapter conclude with any confidence that imperalism is in our future, either in the long term or the short term. But it is true that some of the actions taken on behalf of states, especially by 'strong men' who compare themselves to emperors, czars, and kings, even when they are none of those things, The possible or even probable re-emergence of imperial modes of governance, perhaps best seen in Donald Trump's notions about buying Greenland and taking over Canada as the 51st state, does however provide a good opportunity to clarify just what we mean by 'imperialism' and whether it is the same as 'colonialism'.

Chapter 2 then moves 'downward', so to speak, to the scale of the state, the sovereign. Here we discuss how imperial logics of adding territory and adding popularions that might be ethnically or linguistically novel differ from state-based logics. States, to badly paraphrase Foucault, were born multiple. This is reflected in the structure of the United Nations, where all 130 plus member states are considered as equally sovereign, regardless of size, geographic location, or economic weight.

Chapter 3 focuses on the local, which legally speaking is usually the municipal. Here we warn against taking 'the city' and urban living as the sum total or the microcosm of local governance; rural and suburban populations still exist, and are indeed the majority in some countries, and are arguably entitled to local democracy, just as cities are, according to most urban scholars.

Chapter 4 moves from the 'seeing like a city' scale favoured by urban studies scholars to the smaller, even micro-scale of the 'premium space'. There is a scale of human life that is friendlier and more neighbourly than that of the city. Jane Jacobs, likely the best known of all modern urban studies scholars, famously validated and praised the scale of personal experience, of the part of the urban territory that someone would use in their daily life.

Unfortunately, the rapid rise of gentrified enclaves in inner cities (a phenomenon that Jane Jacobs did not live long enough to fully experience) has meant that resources, public as well as private, have tended to concentrate in certain parts of the city, parts that were already privileged. What is most notable about the rise of what one might call 'premium' spaces is the way in which public resources flow to places that are already enjoying more than their share of private resources. So, city governments (and in this regard cities that are different from rural municipalities, which generally lack gentrified enclaves) – city governments everywhere tend to beautify spaces that are already home to the economically privileged. Flower pots, either hanging from lamp posts or in planters, regularly sprout, along with other features on which public funds have been spent, such as special pavement markings, public art, and flowerbeds. 'Improvements' are made, using public funds and almost always these improvements flow into areas that are already 'nice'. There are legal infrastructures for this process – such as the rise of 'conservancies to govern a particular park, usually in a gentrified or already rich area. Conservancies only increase the social and economic inequality that most contempoorary cities suffer by diverting philanthropic funds to specific areas of the city. As is the case in other situtations, the micro-spaces that are deemed as private or are governed by some specific public-private arrangement sprout in areas that were already preferred by artistic and 'trendy' folks. By contrast, the generic public park is neglected, and appears as more drab by comparison with the new premium spaces.

In Chapters 3, 4 and 5, municipal by-laws are canvassed to show how a legal geography lens – specifically, one informed by empirical research on how marginalized urban denizens actually live and are policed, helps us to understand what is going on and what is the likely future of our urban spaces, and of local government in general. But the point has been made, in the opening paragraphs of this introduction, that in the wake of the 1970s court decisions (in US states and elsewhere) striking down 'status' offences, including vagrancy, as inconsistent with civil/constitutional rights, what has happened is that 'time and space and manner' restrictions have become the authorities' tools of choice.

A typical by-law along these lines, one taken from my knowledge of the city of Toronto's bylaws, but informed by knowledge from many other cities, bans people from selling goods on sidewalks or in parks unless it's during a special festival. The festival is regarded, as Bakhtin said about the carnival, as a time of exception, a time in which closing off streets to motor traffic is permitted, as an exception to the motor vehicle hegemony that contemporary cities labour under.

In general, legal doctrine in common-law jurisdictions tells us that municipalities cannot criminalize anything, the criminal law power being reserved to what are always called 'higher' levels of government. But local authorities can exercise considerable regulatory authority, up to and including expropriating privately owned property.

Chapter 5 is addressed to the scale of the family/household. As feminist geographers and historians of architecture have documented, the normative design of homes, especially the detached homes regarded as best for raising children, contains a whole theory of social and family life. Non-family households often run into legal trouble (not just those households plagued by poverty and disability, but even those young people who prefer to share an apartment with friends rather than spend their whole salary on rent; or retirement homes, as well as group homes, shelters and so on. Prying open the supposed hard wiring that connects forms of housing with the normative 'life stages' of the patriarchal bourgeois nuclear family is the main task of this chapter.

Then follows a chapter that introduces, perhaps for the first time, law students and geography students alike to the lively literature on the human body as a space. Queer theory and feminist geography have plumbed some of the issues that become visible at the scale of the human body, but this type of analysis has largely remained separate, as if it had nothing to say to either law or geography. The hope behind this chapter is that it helps to promote empirical studies that take the human body as the scale of both life and regulation.

Conclusion

Legal geography is especially useful to understand contemporary governance, most especially in cities. Most importantly, legal geography can show us how liberal legal systems have managed to allow authorities including courts to continue punishing 'the usual suspects' but without formal status-based discrimination. Status- or person-based discrimination would make a statute unconstitutional in most Western jurisdictions.

However, the spatial dimension of governance is not wholly unique to municipal or city governance. The migrants that President Trump is currently deporting are also being targeted for being in the wrong place at the wrong time, or perhaps better, with the wrong paperwork.[10] If they remained in Mexico and did not attempt to cross the border north into the United States they would not be bothered (except perhaps by Mexican law enforcement, but not by US officials, who know they have no jurisdiction south of the Mexican border).

There is no hard and fast connection between jurisdictions and ways of seeing, however. A city may for example 'see like a city' when enforcing or not enforcing bylaws, as in the example of the fence viewers given above, but a city can 'see like a state' too when public health inspectors are deployed to check restaurant food safety. The public health inspectors do enforce certain number-driven rules (such as the temperature at which prepared food must be kept, etc.).

Similarly, modern states can also use governing gazes that have little in common with the 'seeing like a state' top-down approach – the rationalistic, survey-centred gaze documented by James Scott. The welfare apparatus of modern capitalist states, for example, has officials who can and sometimes do exercise a more benevolent form of power than 'seeing like a state' suggests.

History cannot be predicted in advance. Even when there is what looks like a 'return' to imperial thinking, the feature being highlighted is never quite

10 In the United States, it is common to talk about 'undocumented' migrants, but this phrase flies in the face of the cumbersome operation of 'Third World' bureaucracies, which produce reams of paper. In Spain the phrase used instead of 'undocumented' is similar – 'sin papeles', without papers. Both phrases make it seem that some people are somehow illegal – as opposed to merely lacking one particular piece of paper such as a a work visa. Working at the Center for Spanish-Speaking Peoples in Toronto (as a volunteer interpreter), years ago, I was amazed by the quantity of documents that so-called illegal 'without-papers' migrants were able to produce – vaccination certificates for their children, marriage certificates, educational certificates, and so on. This experience taught me that so-called undocumented migrants often possess reams of documents.

exactly the same as it had been at the height of nineteenth-century or earlier empires.[11] It is certainly possible that empires will make a comeback, in a new post-Cold War arrangement of alliances and conflicts. But if they do, they will no doubt exhibit different features from previous empires, those of the 'age of exploration' (Portuguese and Spanish, mainly) and those that dominated the nineteenth century and a good part of Africa into the twentieth.[12]

Harvey is an extremely influential geographer, and he has put forward a general theory of the specificity of capitalist imperialism today. Drawing on his earlier work on the way in which capital, especially surplus capital, seeks out novel spaces in which to multiply, he emphasizes the role of spatial expansion – not only expanding into new places (such as the colonies) but also intensifying the capitalist economy, again in various places, some of them new. Ellen Meiksins Wood, an important Marxist theorist of the twentieth century, argued that the older empires of the 'age of exploration' did have capitalist features, but only in certain spaces. Much of the world was not (yet) capitalist. Harvey agrees that capitalism has now become almost universal, or at least world-wide, but he continues to emphasize (as a commitment to the discipline of geography might suggest) capital's search for new and novel spatial 'fixes' (although in recent work Harvey also recognizes that 'fixes' are often also temporal, not only spatial). Anything that stands in the way of capital being invested and producing profits in novel ways is a 'barrier', whether that be a powerful trade union, a set of tariffs, or state measures to regulate the economy.

Harvey's analysis assumes that globalization is an indefinite process; Trump's fondness for tariffs and his clear stance in favour of US national economic gains rather than on global circuits is beyond Harvey's purview. Certainly, in the golden era of neoliberalism (say, the 1980s and 1990s) it was almost impossible to imagine that a new age of tariffs and counter-tariffs would replace the transnational free trade agreements that were so eagerly sought by states in every continent. But one could also see Trump as wanting to pursue an older, imperial, pre-globalization logic, one in which 'the state' acquires a new solidity. He may of course fail. The rest of the world is hardly going to stand by quietly, with various countries tripping over each other to reach special 'deals' with the United States that favour their particular economic make-up. And while individual states may not have either the power or the willingness to antagonize Washington, some coalition may

11 David Harvey, 'In What Ways is the "New Imperialism" Really New?' *Historical Materialism* 15 (2007), 57–70.

12 An influential and equally 'hard Marxist' work along similar lines is Ellen Meiksins Wood, *Empire of Capital* (London, Verso, 2005). Wood, however, is not a geographer; perhaps for that reason she is not so keen on spatial fixes as the way to understand capitalism in the twentieth century.

be in the works even now, as we speak. And of course there are Russia and China, which see themselves as competing empires, each with its own sphere of influence around the world. China is much further along this road than Russia, which in some ways has not yet recovered from the break-up of the Soviet Union and the Soviet bloc.

Whatever happens in the near future (a revival of imperialism, a renaissance of state power, or some combination of the two, perhaps arising from military struggles), the main argument of this book is that legal geography should not be held to be 'best' at any one of the many scales probed in this book. Back in the 1960s the intelligentsia of advanced capitalist countries were faced with a stark choice: either go with the rationalist and numbers-driven appeal of big 'seeing like a state' projects, as New York City's Robert Moses famously did, or else they sided with Jane Jacobs and the 'small is beautiful' approach. Jacobs sang odes to neighbourhoods that functioned as if they were villages. Although she lived first in New York City and then in Toronto, she pioneered a way of seeing life that privileged the scale of the sidewalk – not a generic sidewalk but specific sidewalks, in Greenwich village and then in Toronto's Annex.

Decades after the Moses-Jacobs disputes, and given the rise of social movements that were unknown in the 1960s, it is perhaps a good time to argue for the necessity of multi-scalar approaches. Some of the most innovative citizen-led NGO's work simultaneously at different scales. Food security, for example, is often promoted locally by groups that 'see' the global dimensions of climate change and environmental disaster, but address that by means of local networks through which local farm products reach urban customers, especially in those areas that have become, under agribusiness and oligopolistic grocery stores, food deserts. This book, by showing just a little bit of what becomes visible at each of the scales that mark our daily life, should facilitate both analyses and activisms that do not put different scales or different critical theories in competition against one another, but rather recognize that governance, including governance from below, occurs at many scales at once. Some people will specialize in a certain scale, such as urban homelessness, while others focus on the movement of migrants across oceans and seas. But as we engage with the world's many problems, it is important not to go around promoting the scale that we happen to work at as if it were the 'true' and useful one. Too much damage has been done, to countries, to populations and to social movements, by battles that are fundamentally about scale. Neither Robert Moses nor Jane Jacobs could be a useful slogan for our present. Jane Jacobs has more prestige and a friendlier image than Moses: but one cannot provide electricity or drinking water on a small, neighbourhood scale. What's *under* the sidewalk may have to be planned on a national or regional scale, and that doesn't mean we stop paying attention to bodies, micro-local spaces, cities, states, and empires or would-be empires.

1 Empire as a Scale of Political and Legal Authority

There's a huge amount of both empirical and theoretical work on what many would call 'the modern nation-state', also known as the Westphalian model. Some of this will be canvassed in the next chapter.

'Empire', by contrast, is a term with an old-fashioned ring, evoking early twentieth-century Marxism (which saw imperialism as the latest stage of capitalism) or perhaps the Cold War, during which 'Western' figures such as US President Ronald Reagan identified the Soviet Union as 'the evil empire', and the popular TV show 'West Wing' featured characters who without irony claimed to be working for 'the leader of the free world', meaning of course the president of the United States.

And yet, plenty of research done today, especially in or about the global South, documents the effects and consequences of imperial and colonial relations between the metropole and the countries that have become 'postcolonial', at least formally. I argue here that Empire is indeed a relevant and useful term, especially when contrasted with other scales of political and legal authority.

One sign of the 'revival' of empire talk – a discourse which in some ways competes with 'postcolonial' but in other ways just supplements and updates it – is the largely Marxist discussion of 'the new imperialism'. Drawing on Giovanni Arrighi's earlier work on categories of imperialism, both geographer David Harvey and political scientist Ellen Wood published books, in the early 2000's, arguing that US imperialism is different from the older versions because it is not so much territorial (there aren't actual US colonies, especially if one leaves out Puerto Rico) but rather capitalist. The distinction between territorial imperialism and capitalist imperialism may or may not be helpful to understand what is going on today, but it is important to note it at the outset since it has been utilized by many who are seeking to draw on older Marxist critiques of imperialism as the last or latest stage of capitalism (as Lenin argued) but making an effort to distinguish the largely economic

DOI: 10.4324/9781003612551-2

domination of much of the world by the United States and its corporations from older forms, especially the nineteenth-century British Empire.[1]

One perhaps idiosyncratic place to begin the discussion of imperialism (and its close relative colonialism) is in one of the lecture series that Michel Foucault gave at the College de France, lectures which were eventually published in both French and English many years after his death. The passage that will serve as launching point for this chapter occurs in the course of documenting the genealogy and the logic of the very French notion of 'raison d'etat'.

The phrase 'raison d'Etat' is seldom used in English. And yet it should be familiar, since it indicates the rationale that is used to justify national security apparatuses' coexistence with a theoretically liberal legal system. In a world context in which democracy is often undermined by authoritarian rulers, it is worthwhile to return, however briefly, to the question of 'Empire' as a distinct logic of governance, one that covers both colonialism and imperialism.

In an aside that has great potential but remains undeveloped by Foucault himself, and by his many followers, he notes that the modern nation-state was born in the plural form.[2]

Foucault's analysis of the genealogy of modern European states should not be read as a general 'theory' of the difference between empire and nation-state. For one thing, like everything else in Foucault's work, the analysis is tied to a particular time and space. In his earlier work Foucault focuses on Europe in the shift from medieval political imaginations to what historians of Europe call the Renaissance and Reformation[3] – the era that Foucault called the 'classical' era.

In the context of an analysis of the demise of the medieval notion of a 'last' Empire, imagined as inaugurated by a second coming of Christ (or sometimes as the world dominance of a pan-Christian, pan-European empire, perhaps the successor to the Holy Roman Empire, which was not much of an empire and was certainly not holy – or Roman, for that matter). In a discussion mainly focused on the emergence of 'raison d'Etat' as a modern logic of political authority, Foucault makes a throwaway remark about 'Empire' as a scale

1 David Harvey, *The New Imperialism* (Oxford University Press, 2003) and Ellen Meiksins Wood, *Empire of Capital* (London, Verso, 2005).

2 The relevant passage is found in the published transcript of Foucault's lecture at the College de France given on March 15, 1978. The lecture series, known in the Anglosphere as the 'governmentality' lectures, were published under the title *Security, Territory, Population: Lectures at the College de France 1977–78* (transl. Graham Burchell), New York: Picador 2007. The passage cited here is on p. 260 of the English translation.

3 For a longer explanation of why Foucault should not be read as a 'theorist', much less a philosopher, see Mariana Valverde, *Michel Foucault* (London, Routledge, 2017).

of political authority, a remark that is not followed up either empirically or theoretically.[4]

The absence of a systematic analysis of empire in Foucault's work is odd, considering the fact that Foucault's teen years were marked by the French war against Algerian independence, and the further fact that Foucault lived in Tunis for some time (fortunately or unfortunately being in Tunis and missing out on the May of 1968 events in Paris as a result[5]). The emphasis is on the centralization and unification of political authority under the 'empire' diagram of political power. Whether he would agree with Steinmetz that empires are generally militarized is unknown; it may be that militarization is just as much a feature of modern nation-states as of Empires with serious armies.[6]

That unification drive and centralization of power is contrasted to the inherently plural character of the Westphalian 'system', which has as its foundation mutual respect for other (European and Christian) sovereigns, whose territory is meant to be 'theirs' – as is the case in the contemporary UN, where respect for each country's sovereignty is the most important principle.

In general, Foucault has little to say throughout his work about imperialism and colonialism. His work is therefore not the obvious point from which to launch a legal geography of empire and colonialism. His familiarity with the former French colonies in North Africa undoubtedly helped him develop his well-known analysis of the constitutive role of racism in modern

4 US legal sociologist George Steinmetz, whose expertise is mainly in the little-studied (in English-speaking circles) German Empire, wrote that 'empire is the overarching concept in all discussions of imperialism and colonialism'. He then offers the generalization that empires tend to be 'expansive, militarized [and] multi-ethnic' (G. Steinmetz, 'The sociology of empires, colonies, and postcolonialism' *Annual Review of Sociology* vol. 14 (2014), pages 2 and 3). Decades ago anthropologists, in a fit of collective reflexivity, pointed out that the notion of 'the primitive' was highly problematic and Eurocentric. The assigning of the 'primitive' or the 'savage' to anthropology took place just as sociology emerged as the science of modern, civilized societies. Anthropology abandoned the 'primitive' and 'savage' categories. By contrast, sociologists seldom acknowledge that if the 'primitive' must be thrown on the garbage heap of history, so is its binary opposite, modernity. The most interesting theorizations of eurocentrism and empire have come from historians (such as Dipesh Chakrabarty, in his magnum opus *Provincializing Europe* [Princeton University Press, 2000]).

5 The passage cited here is in Michel Foucault, *Security, Territory Population: lectures at the College de France, 1977–78* (transl. Graham Burchell; New York, Picador, 2010), p. 260. For Foucault's travels as a cultural diplomat, to Tunis and to Poland, see Didier Eribon, *Michel Foucault* (orig. French edition Paris, Flammarion, 1989; English translation Cambridge MA, Harvard University Press, 1992).

6 The current Trump administration is chastising NATO member states for not pulling their weight in terms of military spending. Contrary to many of the outright lies told by Trump, it is true that many smaller nation-states have come to rely on the United States Army (and Navy, and Air Force). That perhaps is a symptom of lingering or newly reactivated imperial power; traditionally colonies did not maintain their own armies – and neither did Germany, until recently; the country was for many years occupied by foreign military forces.

biopolitics[7]. But the 'race' and 'racism' that appear in Foucault's work[8] are not the notions – many of them taking the United States as paradigm instance – best articulated by contemporary Critical Race Theory, but rather mostly as a way to explain how 'negative' biopolitics (what we would now call, following African theorist Achille Mbembe, necropolitics) can coexist with biopolitical projects that seek to improve the human resources of a population. 'Positive' biopolitical projects I call those projects such as as near-universal vaccination or other public health measures. 'Negative' biopolitics, by contrast, is more coercive, often seeking to eliminate from what is often called 'the national lifeblood' impure and/or foreign elements. The Nazi destruction of Jews and Eastern European Slavic peoples, along with other 'undesirables' (the Nazi phrase 'lives not worth living' is telling) is the best known example of 'negative' biopolitics.

In that remark about 'Empire', one of the few places in his works where empire is even mentioned, Foucault mentions that the logic of Empire is unifying, and in fact depends on and implements a unified approach to political authority.

This seems insightful, despite its lack of engagement with Fanon and other global South theorists (though few of them were available to Foucault at the time). Ever since the Roman Empire, Empire is or seeks to be all-encompassing, expanding as much as possible, taking in more and more territory and absorbing different populations. The populations may remain distinct culturally but what one could call the idea of Empire is to subject these populations (whether assimilated or left in a relatively autonomous situation) to a central and in most cases distant sovereign.

7 Ann Laura Stoler and many other writers (often combining postcolonial studies and interpretations of Foucault) have done a great deal for several decades now to show how Foucault's work can be useful for historians of empire and of racism. A.L. Stoler, *Race and the Education of Desire* (1995) was a formative early work attempting to utilize Foucault, especially his then not yet published lectures, for critical analyses of empire. For a recent contribution to this lively debate see Claire Cosquer, 'Altering Absence: From Race to Empire in Readings of Foucault' *Foucault Studies* vol. 26 (June 2019), pp. 1–20. We can expect that over the next decade or so the relatively new field of 'Black geography' will be taken up by people engaged in legal geography research. Critical work on empire and law has flourished most strongly amongst historians of the British Empire, especially South Asia, and they in turn tend to neglect African-American work in cultural studies and geography. On their part US-based critical race theory authors tend to neglect the transnational. The isolation of different disciplines, and the pressures on younger scholars to publish in leading discipline-based journals, have arguably prevented the emergence of any synthesis of global-south postcolonial studies and US-centered work on anti-Black racism.

8 Especially in the 1975–1976 lecture series published as *Society Must Be Defended* (transl. David Macey), New York: Picador (London, St. Martin's Press, 2003). The French original was published in Paris in 1997. For the reading of 'race' and Foucault's interest in 'the war of the races' in European history see Mariana Valverde, 'Genealogies of European States: Foucaultian Reflections' *Economy and Society* vol. 36, 1 (2007), 159–178.

By contrast, the so-called Westphalian 'system', which with the 1648 Treaty of Westphalia attempted to put an end to the centuries-old wars of religion in Europe, presupposed that nation-states were plural. One of the expected outcomes of the Treaty of Westphalia was that religious wars in Europe could be avoided and prevented if there was a pragmatic agreement among sovereign nations that the faith of the sovereign was automatically the faith of his or her subjects, at least officially. Hence, there need be no more 'Hundred Years' War'. Of course the vast majority of sovereigns were male. But the well-documented British tensions between the Catholic daughter of Henry VIII, Mary, and his Protestant daughter, Elizabeth, well known to TV viewers through the historical show 'the Tudors', make the 'he or she' phrasing relevant in British history.

Given the inter-Christian pluralism created in and/or following the Reformation, a way to prevent future wars between European sovereigns (in the aftermath of the so-called Hundred Years' War) was sought. The fiction that everyone who was a subject of a particular sovereign shared the sovereign's faith became a necessary technique for preventing inter-European wars after the Treaty of Westphalia in 1648.[9]

Existing historical work on different empires, from the Roman Empire to the Austro-Hungarian Empire (which extended from the seventeenth-century Habsburg dynasty to 1918), supports Foucault's rather idle comments. In general we can say that historical scholarship has established that while the newly secured nation-states had great difficulty in dealing with internal divisions, especially along religious (Protestant vs Catholic, mainly) lines, empires were far more tolerant of national, racial, cultural and religious diversity. There was no assumption of a common ethnicity, a common religion or even a common language, in the large multi-ethnic empires that flourished in Asia and in Europe (East and West) from the fall of the Roman Empire. The Byzantine empire, for example, which began life as the eastern sector of the Roman Empire but evolved into its own political unit, was notoriously multicultural.

The Roman Empire, in turn, had allowed newly conquered nations to retain their traditional gods (as Foucault would have known from his friend and colleague Paul Veyne, a respected historian of the European Roman Empire). In turn, the Austro-Hungarian Empire, like the temporally overlapping Ottoman Empire, did not attempt to institute either cultural/religious or ethnic uniformity. One could be Czech but live more or less happily under the 'K und K' empire (the Austro-Hungarian empire, that is, with K and K referring to 'king' and 'emperor' in German).

In the Habsburg empire, one could be ethnically Polish but speak the common language of the empire, German, as some of my ancestors did, who

9 The Wikipedia entry for 'Westphalian system' is reasonably accurate and helpful, for those without sufficient background in European political history (accessed January 7, 2025).

were Polish but possessed bibles and other books in German that have been passed down to their Spanish descendants. The descendants in Spain were the eventual fruit of an internal Habsburg empire alliance whereby a sort-of-noble Polish lady with a German-language title married a Basque/Spanish gentleman.

I happen to know a bit about the Habsburg empire via family stories, since my own grandfather, Wilhelm Gefaell, a Viennese Jew, had an Austro-Hungarian empire passport when he moved to Spain around 1910. My mother once showed me the actual passport, although its whereabouts are not known, to me at least. The passport became a serious inconvenience in 1914: since the home country of the hydroelectric company for which he worked in Spain as an engineer was Canada, which went to war with Austro-Hungary starting in 1914 (following the British lead), my grandfather was forced to leave his job – he was an enemy alien from the Canadian and British point of view.

An interesting anecdote that illustrates the games that individuals can play with or against plural sovereigns is that later on, during the Spanish Civil War, in 1937 or 1938, my grandfather managed to parlay his symbolic diplomatic status as the honorary consul of Austria (he must have obtained an Austrian passport after the empire fell in 1918, replaced by various nation-states including Austria) into a practical service to his ten-children family.

The whole family-based household, including several servants as well as the ten children, was transported from one part of the Basque country that had become controlled by left-wing Republican forces to another more conservative part. This was deemed prudent since during the war the family were firmly on Franco's side. The move, which had to be by sea due to ongoing battles and well-defined trenches on land, was carried out by none other than the Nazi navy, flying the swastika flag (as my mother recalled to me, a childhood memory on her part since she was about eight years old at the time). The utilization of a weak diplomatic status (honorary consuls are not exactly official diplomats) to facilitate a family emergency trip, on a Nazi ship, despite the family being half-Jewish and the pater familias being all Jewish, demonstrated a certain agility.

The game of jurisdiction is usually played between states, but at times individuals with plural or mixed identities can also play the game. Many in his family in Vienna fell victim to the Nazis, eventually. But unlike his mother and his sisters, who were victims of the Holocaust, Wilhelm was able to utilize imperial and national belonging to his personal advantage, in that particular instance of the trip by sea.

Of course, he was not always able to be a winner in the game of political identities. As just mentioned, he was unable to play the game of jurisdiction to his own advantage when he lost his engineering job with the electricity company known in Spanish history as 'La Canadiense'. And he fared even worse when after failing to persuade his aged and blind mother in Vienna to move to Spain, when the Civil War ended and the family returned to Madrid, his sisters and his mother fell victim to the Nazi Holocaust. I have in my possession a postcard (no doubt postcards had become mandatory in international mail by then, to facilitate the task for the Nazi censors) where his one remaining brother in Vienna intimates that their mother has 'disappeared', but without mentioning any details.

But when the Nazi ship (or submarine, my mother did not remember the nautical details, not surprisingly because she could never tell one brand of car from another) took his family, in 1937 or 1938, to a politically safer space. Clearly then he was certainly playing the game of jurisdiction to his advantage, with the Nazis – the ones on the ship but also the larger Nazi government in Berlin – being succesfully fooled.

My mother told me (in the 1980s, when Jewish ancestry had changed cultural status significantly since the immediate post-World War II period) that her father gave strict travel instructions to his ten kids to only speak German during the short trip by sea. His older daughters could speak German reasonably well, and no doubt the good-looking teen girls were a sight for sore eyes for the German sailors and were likely chatted up all the way. The reason for the language requirement that my grandfather thought was necessary (although he may have been wrong on that) was that he thought he had to maintain the fiction that the whole family was Austrian, not Spanish, in order to utilize his status as honorary consul to advantage. In those days young readers will not remember, the father's nationality determined both that of his wife and that of his children. My grandfather Wilhelm had become a de facto right-wing Spaniard, and is thus buried near Madrid in the 'family' cemetery plot where other relatives are also buried. His skeleton lies under a headstone that reads 'Guillermo' (not Wilhelm) Gefaell Feil – as if his mother's maiden name were his second last name, which would be the case in Spain.

Apparently he complained all his life that Spanish people used olive oil in every dish consumed, and said that he did not want to be buried in his wife's family plot. But he remained in Spain, never going back to Vienna even after World War II was over. And during World War II he even did business in Nazi Germany for a patent company based in Madrid that employed him (and likely valued the fact that he spoke fluent German).

But let us leave my relatives to one side and go back to what 'Empire' might mean as a scale of political authority. In thinking about empire, one might want to identify the features of the European empires of the early modern period, which due to a systematic lack of bureaucratic state capacity (by comparison with nineteenth-century empires) and an equally striking lack of large military active-duty forces (imperial soldiers had to be paid, often in advance) could only engage in imperial ventures if those desires were made effective by chartered companies enjoying quasi-sovereign as well as landowner status: the Dutch East India Company or VOC, the British East India Company, and the Hudson's Bay company in North America, as well as Portuguese and German companies operating in Africa. These empires were dependent on the 'company-states' which did much the dirty work of colonization, and so those empires are arguably different from the later, more territorially and militarily oriented empires, primarily the British Empire in its heyday in the nineteenth century.

Comparative studies of different empires are very rare, however, so any generalizations are risky. Certainly the nineteenth-century empires were all far more bureaucratized and verbose than earlier ones. Patrick Joyce's reflections on the efforts made by London-based officials attempting to read the reams of correspondence from well-educated gentlemen in India who apparently had little to do but write dispatches 'home' are telling.[10] Other studies too have identified growing bureaucratization as a key trend in nineteenth-century and early twentieth-century empires. Prior to the 1920s or 1930s few European states had anything like modern bureaucracies, and as a result, empires too were greatly shaped by the presence or absence of a bureaucracy such as the India Office in London.

In Foucault's 'classical' period – which British and French historians would call 'early modern Europe' – states were largely dependent on the company-states that had been created by royal charter. Lack of a state bureaucracy was not the only reason for relying on company-states. Chartering a company that was both owner of land and sovereign or quasi-sovereign in the territory was the only practical way one could create a corporate person, before general incorporation statutes for both public corporations such as municipalities and business enterprises became popular.

The 'classical' empires (in the sense of having flourished in the 'classical' era) are arguably substantially different from the nineteenth-century European powers best known for the 'scramble for Africa' of the late nineteenth century (a scramble supposedly settled by the Berlin conference of 1885, but reactivated during World War I). Those differences make any generalizations about 'empire' questionable – which is perhaps the most important lesson one can draw from Foucault's work taken as a whole, since he always eschewed defining concepts, and would not have wanted to pursue a conceptual exploration of 'state' vs. 'empire.'

But one can say, by way of a quasi-generalization, that the French, the German and the British Empires of the mid and late nineteenth century (the main 'scramble for Africa' protagonists) were all based on the assumption that the culture (and the law) of the 'home' country, the metropole, could and should be extended to the colonies. This was meant to be especially the case for the settler colonies, but not only them. The earlier empires were, as has been mentioned, dependent on the personnel and the legal, practical, and military work of the chartered companies that acted, in historian Philip Stern's

10 Patrick Joyce, *The State of Freedom: A social history of the British State since 1800* (Cambridge University Press, 2013), chapter 4 ('Filing the Raj'), pp. 144–184.

famous phrase, as 'company-states'.[11] And these companies, mostly focused on the bottom line, rarely sought to impose the law of the metropole in far-off colonies that served mainly as a source of natural resources, or else used the law of the 'home' country only to regulate disputes between employees.

The British nineteenth-century Empire, which has a vast and sophisticated historiography, was nevertheless based on the practice of sending educated English gentlemen to far-off destinations to rule, or try to rule, over the 'natives'. That particular empire also encouraged Christian missions, along with occasional tolerance for pre-existing belief systems.[12] But the British Empire, to generalize, was less tolerant of cultural and linguistic diversity than the Austro-Hungarian or the Ottoman Empire – never mind the Roman Empire. Law figured rather centrally in British imperialism: even when traditional Indigenous law was tolerated, however, it had a subordinate status, with major criminal cases being handled by British courts.[13] The somewhat mythical ideal of 'British justice' was certainly a major technique of imperial domination.[14]

A notable absence not only in Foucault's work but in much of the contemporary work on British colonialism, the literature that has seen the most

11 Philip Stern, *The Company-State: Corporate sovereignty and the early modern foundations of the British Empire in India (*New York,Oxford University Press, 2011). Also see George Steinmetz, *The Devil's Handwriting: Precoloniality in Qindao, Samoa and Southwest Africa* (University of Chicago Press, 2007). Paul Rabinow's pioneering work on urban design in French North Africa is also illuminating and has been heavily cited: Paul Rabinow, *French Modern: Forms and Norms of the Social Environment* (Chicago, University of Chicago Press, 1995). Paying special attention to architecture and urban design, Rabinow does begin to offer a legal geography of Empire.

12 European women played an important but often unacknowledged role, especially in the British Empire, where they often ran mission schools and orphanages. The earlier Spanish Empire in Latin America was not keen on white Spanish women participating in any imperial ventures, even as wives of the white settlers. One might say that the absence of imported white European women helped to foster the ideology of 'metissage' or racial hybridity that is so dear to Latin American official state ideologies, including those of Mexico and Brazil. See inter alia Edward Telles and Denia Garcia, '"Mestizaje" and Public Opinion in Latin America' *Latin American Research Review* vol. 48 no. 3 (2013), 130–152.

13 The literature that from the 1960s onward documented the awkward coexistence of Indigenous and imperial law in eighteenth and nineteenth century empires is known in socio-legal studies circles as 'legal pluralism'. Many anthropologists, mainly of European origin, have written about legal pluralism and have documented its contradictions, but there are legal scholars who have contributed to this field as well, such as Teemu Ruskola ('Legal Orientalism', *University of Michigan Law Review* vol. 101 (2002). See also the blog 'Everyday Orientalisms', which continues these conversations in the present, with particular attention to Palestine (https://everydayorientalism.wordpress.com/)

14 Evidence for the power of the 'British justice' ideology is found in numerous studies of the British Empire by legal historians. For an overview of the insanity defense in imperial context, see Catherine Evans, *Unsound Empire: Civilization and Madness in Late Victorian Law* (New Haven CT, Yale University Press, 2021).

lively debates about the legal aspects of imperialism and colonialism, is the longest lasting empire in history – the Chinese Empire. The Chinese Empire, which arguably has resuscitated in recent years, well after the Mao Tse Tung Communist period, has periodically cultivated an official image of multiculturalism. It is hard to say whether the Chinese state is now (early 2025) more of an empire or more of a nation-state; but either way, Chinese citizens are regularly exposed to televised performances of 'ethnic' minority dancing and singing, played on national TV during official celebrations. Whether those are more like the Soviet-era demonstrations of the ability of a strong nation-state to value the culture of minority groups (only the culture, often reified as 'colourful native costume') or more like shows of imperial might is not easy to discern.

Further, some Chinese state policies have provided a kind of affirmative action for ethnic minority groups. Ethnic minorities, for example, were exempt from the harshly enforced one-child law, when it was in force for the majority Han Chinese population.

The Soviet Union too claimed to be multi-cultural and multi-faith, tolerating Islam in many of its constituent republics. It is true that the Soviet Union did not see itself as a continuation of the czarist empire. By contrast, today, in post-Soviet Russia, Putin does not hesitate to praise the Orthodox Russian Church, which had been censored and discriminated against during the Communist period. Putin also loves to engage in other common modern nation-building exercises, from waging offensive wars through physically eliminating enemies of the Kremlin to hosting Olympic games.

The process by which a nation-state that used to be an empire might regain its imperial mantle has not been studied, perhaps because one would need some distance from current events. China may be on the road to a new Empire as well as Russia. In general, though, there's an agreement, best represented by the UN, that the world system we have now is a system of sovereign states where imperial ventures are frowned upon.[15]

What Is Imperialism?

Imperialism is often seen as more of an economic phenomenon than anything else. It was first theorized as a late stage of world capitalism by Lenin and others such as the British journalist John A. Hobson, who published a full-length work in 1902 on imperialism as the latest stage of capitalism. Not surprisingly, subsequent theories of imperialism have developed mainly within

15 As soon as President Trump was inaugurated for his second term (January 20, 2025) he made a lot of noise about buying Greenland from Denmark, taking over the Panama Canal, and turning Canada into the 'fifty-first state'. These threats were not welcomed anywhere outside of Trump world but they still dominated headlines well into Trump's second term.

a Marxist framework (from Rosa Luxemburg in the 1910s to Andre Gunder Frank and international-development 'dependency' theorists in the 1960s and beyond).

But politically and legally, imperialism can be characterized as political authority exercised at a distance. This often happens as the dominant power recruits local elites and sets up secondary, subordinate centres of power, in industrial branch plants, economic and social enclaves with special rules, and the like. Diplomatic personnel as well as various security forces (such as the American Drug Enforcement Agency) may also be heavily involved in such a way that the less powerful country feels like Americans are 'the boss' in all manner of situations.

One can certainly talk about American imperialism existing today in Central and South America. The coups d'etat that the United States has facilitated in the region for well over a century were not usually direct American military interventions (with a couple of notable exceptions, namely the marines landing on Santo Domingo in the 1960s and the later US army takeover of Grenada). By and large, American interventions were not undertaken with a view to establishing new colonies. There were usually local military leaders and/or business magnates (including notorious dictators, such as Augusto Somoza in Nicaragua and Gen. Augusto Pinochet in Chile) who rebelled against or sought to prevent regimes seen as too liberal or socialist.

Thus, in what could be seen as a revival of the British policy in colonial Africa of 'indirect rule', local actors, corporate and military, were generally willing to facilitate American interference in their domestic affairs. Many Latin American criminologists, for example, believe that American policies on illegal drugs have shaped national legal and policing efforts in Latin America, to the detriment of policies that are more responsive to local conditions, and perhaps less keen on the myth that one can just 'say no to drugs'.

The military dictatorships that blighted twentieth-century Latin American history (in Nicaragua, El Salvador, Uruguay, Argentina, Brasil and Chile) were opposed by guerrilla groups and other resistance forces that targeted not only local dictators but American imperialism. The resistance movements thus usually took on a nationalistic and anti-imperialist flavour. That was the case in Cuba when Fidel Castro and his small band of armed men managed to prevail against the Batista dictatorship (in the 1950s). The charismatic figure of Che Guevara has served for many years to promote this mixture of nationalism and anti-imperialism. (In Cuba one can still buy the classic t-shirt featuring Che Guevara's image, often manipulated to make him look like the dead Jesus Christ.)

A similar mixture of political motives, nationalistic and anti-imperialist, can be seen today amongst many Palestinians, in Palestine and the diaspora. By virtue of the continous US funding of the Israeli armed forces, Palestinians at home and also in the diaspora feel they should target both the Israeli state and the US government in their protests. Since Israel claims to be the true home of Jews the world over it is not exactly an imperialist power; but many Palestinians would argue that it is a settler colonial state, since it has, since 1948, sought to replace the Indigenous Palestinians with Jews, often refugees or immigrants from Europe.

One can also talk cogently about the imperialism that was fuelled by anti-communism during the Cold War – exemplified in what political scientists and Cold War experts call 'proxy wars'. A *proxy war* is one where small countries such as Mozambique, Iraq, Afghanistan or Syria are more or less forced to line up with one superpower, or with its enemy.

Currently, the ongoing war in Ukraine (as of early 2025) can be described as a Cold War revival. The Ukranian army relies heavily on arms and ammunition and training provided by the United States and by its European allies in NATO. Whether Russian aggression in Ukraine is best seen as the revival of the Russian empire of the czars or as the building of a post-Soviet autocratic Russian nation-state is for area experts to decide – likely after some years have gone by. But because we tend to focus on the decline of empires (ever since Gibbon's massive work on the decline of the Roman Empire, much read in nineteenth- and even twentieth-century Britain) does not mean that new or re-invented empires cannot be born. As the philosopher Hegel said, the conceptual framing for an era can only be seen, by philosophers at any rate, after the fact. 'The owl of Minerva' (the philosophical bird), in Hegel's famous phrase, 'only spreads its wings with the falling of the dark'.

Imperialism, nevertheless, has meant that one hegemonic, dominant country – whose economy and whose currency dominate what is called 'the global economy' – exercises power well beyond its legal borders, most often through economic links. That in February of 2025 both Mexico and Canada, as well as China, are facing the threat of Trump's 25% tariffs, shows just how powerful American imperialism is (although many speculate that the threat will remain a threat but not become real policy.)

By contrast to today, in the days (say 1820s to 1920s) when the sun literally did not set on the British Empire,[16] the pound sterling was the main currency of international trade, and the 'City' (London's financial centre) was the main global marketplace, including for infrastructure projects in far-off countries. If one wanted to seek financing for a project such as the Suez Canal, or a railway in South America, one went to London, specifically to 'the City' (the one square mile around the Bank of England, which even today is its

16 British imperialists at home and abroad were fond of saying that due to the global spread of the Empire, the sun never set on it (since when it set in one country it was shining in another that was equally dependent on Britain).

own municipality, the Corporation of the City of London, with its own police force).[17]

As the twentieth century wore on, and especially after World War II, which was economically highly beneficial for the US, the United States came to replace Britain. The New York Stock Exchange and the Wall Street financial firms and private equity funds are now the centre of world finance, having to a large extent replaced London's 'City'. The fact that Britain's economy was in literal ruins after the war, while the US economy remained more or less untouched and the US government 'helped' Britain with loans that had to be repaid in the immediate postwar period – a period which in the UK was marked by shortages, rationing and austerity, in part because of the huge financial debt owed to the United States – was certainly a key moment in a sort of baton transfer from one empire to its successor.

As mentioned above, it is not yet possible to say whether China or Russia or both are also imperalist or neo-imperialist. Clearly they, or rather their rulers, have ambitions in that direction. And yet the fact that British colonies came to be regarded by the London masters, eventually, as a money pit rather than an asset is likely to act as a warning lesson for today's would-be empires. The Chinese government's Belt and Road Initiative, combining infrastructure with finance (loans owed to Chinese state entities) in classic imperialist fashion has arguably created a whole new 'empire' in South Asia and Africa, or at least a Chinese sphere of influence.

As part of the Chinese quest for imperial or quasi-imperial power, logistics-oriented container ports have been financed and sometimes built by Chinese state-owned corporations. And Chinese mining companies are busy entering into 'partnerships' with relatively weak governments from Malaysia to Canada.[18] But only the future will tell us whether China's role in parts of the world largely abandoned by the European and American empires constitutes a new type of empire or rather a new type of authoritarian state.

What Is Colonialism?

It is easy to confuse imperialism with colonialism. But colonialism, which goes back to the ancient Romans and Greeks, since both of these centres of power established colonies all through the Mediterranean, is different from

17 On the shift from British to American domination, see Julian Go, *Patterns of Empire: the British and American Empires 1688 to the Present* (Cambridge, Cambridge University Press, 2011).

18 On the logistics industry and the proliferation of container-driven securitized ports, see Deborah Cowen, *The Deadly Life of Logistics: Mapping Violence in Global Trade* (Minneapolis, University of Minnesota Press, 2014).

economic domination – although it can certainly coexist with it, and usually does.

Colonialism involves creating new populations or subjugating existing populations by means of processes that are diverse but all huddle under the umbrella term 'colonization'. Within the American empire, there is an unease about the arguably colonial status of territories such as Puerto Rico or the US Virgin Islands, which are 'territories' and hence lack representation in Congress (in Puerto Rico there is a strong nationalist movement that seeks to become the 51st state, which would mean congressional representation and the federal presidential suffrage).

When settlers from the metropole go abroad to found colonies, as the ancient Romans and Greeks did, new populations are created. The so-called 'pieds noirs' that France saw as a means to prolong its colonialism in northern Africa (who were ethnically French but lived and in some cases were born in Africa) are an example from the mid-twentieth century. The pieds-noirs (so called because they had their feet in Africa, not because they were Black) returned to France en masse once North African colonies from Algiers to Morocco achieved independence, in the late 1950s and early 1960s. (In fact some scholars say that France did not become a proper modern nation state until 1962, since only in that year did Algeria obtain independence).

Not much later, France lost Indochina, as Southeast Asia was called back when it was French (French Indochina was what is now Vietnam plus a few other territories). This loss was due to some particular causes but also to the world-wide eruption of the anti-colonial, anti-racist nationalism, within which *Franz Fanon* was arguably the most important intellectual force.

The literature on colonialism – modern colonialism, not the ancient forms that gave rise to 'colonies' along many Mediterranean shores, from southern France to Turkey – suggests that it is important, politically as well as intellectually, to distinguish the two main kinds of colonialism. One is the direct form of rule whose best known example is India during the Raj, on the one hand; on the other hand we see elsewhere the less direct and usually slower and often more legalistic and partly benevolent or paternalistic path known as settler colonialism.

Not all colonialism is of the settler variety, therefore. This needs to be emphasized, despite the fact that in some countries 'settler colonial studies' has emerged with great prestige and has in some cases overshadowed other forms of postcolonial thought and practice. Canada, Australia, New Zealand and the early United States (before 1776) were British settler colonies.[19] *Settler colonialism* means a wholesale transfer of populations (often achieved

19 For a rare but influential application of settler colonial analyses to the early United States, see Christopher Tomlins, *Freedom Bound: Law, Labor and Civic identity in Colonial English America 1580–1865* (Cambridge University Press, 2010), especially the first few chapters.

in part by creating crises, such as the Irish potato famine, which pushed people out of the metropole/Europe)[20] and the replacement of Indigenous populations by settlers, that is, in the case of Britain, English, Scottish, Irish and Welsh people.

In Ontario, where I live, the British military authorities engaged in the task of surveying the land (land mostly stolen from Indigenous peoples, of course) and decided to build what were called at the time, with zero irony, 'colonization' roads. These were often literally drawn with rulers on paper maps in relatively distant Toronto – the reason why so many 'back' roads in Ontario have huge hills that pose serious winter driving risks.

Unlike roads emerging from actual travel, either by animals or humans, which predominate in Europe, the mostly ruler-straight 'colonization' roads found in a large part of Ontario were the product of the kind of imagination that James Scott famously called 'Seeing like a state'.[21] Or perhaps the roads in rural Ontario were examples of 'seeing like an empire', a gaze for governing Others that Scott does not differentiate from seeing like a state.

The settlers of settler colonialism, in all cases, had a strong sense of cultural superiority. This meant that there were hierarchies classifying different kinds of European immigrants as more or less desirable depending on their perceived cultural specifities.[22] But a key element was that the settler mentality regarded Indigenous populations as 'vanishing races' destined to disappear. (Indeed, the phrase 'vanishing race' was very popular, including in European writing about imagined Indigenous peoples – literature of the 'last of the Mohicans' variety.)

And importantly for law, what came to be known as 'British justice' in the Empire was an integral component of this feeling of superiority.[23] Especially after the United States obtained its independence by force of arms, the semi-colonial regime in Canada, prided itself, as is still the case today, in its differentiation from the republic to the south, and the fact that there was no

20 Patrick Scanlan, *Rot: An Imperial History of the Irish Famine* (New York, Basic Books, 2025). This book situates the 'potato famine' within the context of British imperial and colonial goals, especially that of creating a 'modern' capitalist economy in Ireland, which never worked. But as Foucault said about the prison, a widespread realization that a particular 'solution' does not work as promised does not necessarily means it is abandoned.

21 James C Scott, *Seeing Like a State: How Projects to Improve the Human Condition Have Failed.*

22 A notable Canadian example is the 1910 book by a noted founder of social democracy in Canada, the Protestant minister from Winnipeg J.S. Woodsworth – *Our Neighbour* (orig. pub. 1911). This book, used in early Canadian sociology classes, contains the then routine hierarchical classification of immigrants and potential immigrants, with northern Europeans at the top and Asian and Black migrants at the bottom.

23 On the notion of 'British justice' in action, see Barrington Walker, *Race on trial: Black defendants in Canadian criminal courts 1858–1968* (Toronto, University of Toronto Press, 2010), and Catherine Evans, *Unsound Empire: Madness and the law in the late Victorian Empire* (New Haven, Yale University Press, 2015).

legalized slavery in Canada served to perpetuate the notion that British justice was superior, more Christian and more rational, than American justice.

The Canadian state project of Indian Residential Schools is an internationally known project of settler colonialism. Widespread publicity about the residential schools, especially the findings of the national Truth and Reconciliation Commission that reported in 2015, has served to educate many everyday Canadians on the meaning and significance of 'settler colonialism'. Most Canadians now would heartily disagree with the language used by the top bureaucrat in charge of 'Indian Affairs' in the early twentieth century, who said that the residential schools, to which 'Indian' children were sent with or without parental consent, were meant to 'kill the Indian in the child'.

The residential school project was dubbed by the official Truth and Reconciliation Commission reporting in 2015 as 'cultural genocide' – a phrase that many Canadians have disavowed, but others have embraced. Many Indigenous people in Canada, increasingly aware of the slower but state-facilitated violence perpetrated systematically first by the French Empire, the British Empire and then by the Canadian state, call the residential school project (which survived into the late twentieth century) genocide tout court.[24]

The settler colonial frame persisted into 1969, when Pierre Trudeau and his Minister for 'Indian Affairs' Jean Chretien (who later became Prime Minister) issued a 'white paper' (policy discussion paper) that suggested, in keeping with many earlier Canadian state projects, that the movement of history was such that 'Indians' would slowly disappear as a distinct legal category, their children becoming increasingly assimilated into white settler Canadian society. One could say that the line between cultural genocide and actual genocide is not easy to draw, therefore.

But genocide is not always a preferred strategy of colonialism. The Spanish Empire in the Americas, for example, did engage in and facilitate many racist killings, and facilitated the wholesale enslavement of Africans. Nevertheless, whether because there were too many Indigenous people in the Spanish-controlled Americas (as compared to places such as Australia and Canada) or for other reasons, most of the population of Latin America is today a mixture of Indigenous and Spanish (or other European) 'blood'. Many Latin Americans also have African roots, due to the prevalence for a couple of centuries of enslaved Black people, especially in Brazil and in the West Indian sugar, spice and rum islands.

In the nineteenth century – perhaps the golden age of Empire, or maybe only of the British Empire – the most important colony held by Britain (the 'jewel in the imperial Crown') was universally said to be India. India, which during its colonial era included Pakistan and Bangla Desh), was the 'crown

24 One could reflect on the historical precedents for contemporary news coverage about Ukranian children being removed to Russia. For children as a transnational currency, see Karen Dubinsky, *Babies Without Borders: Adoption and Migration Across the Americas* (Toronto, University of Toronto Press, 2010).

jewel', and in fact was not dubbed a colony in official discourse. Queen Victoria was crowned Empress of India, interestingly in her absence.[25]

After that, the imperial Crown was physically and legally separate from the British Crown. Interestingly, both Crowns, in their distinct jewelled materialities, were placed on Queen Elizabeth's coffin during her state funeral in 2023, as YouTube video of the funeral – which was arguably a monument to imperialism – shows. At the judicial level the highest authority on British imperial law was the selection of Law Lords constituted as the Judicial Committee of the Privy Council.[26]

The two terms, *imperialism* and *colonialism*, are therefore not synonymous. Often, people talk about 'colonialism' but they mean imperialism – as when Latin Americans complain about the oversized influence of the US government on domestic matters such as policies and laws on illegal drugs. The 20 or so Latin American republics were once colonies within the Spanish Empire.

The Spanish empire, however, was never keen on settler colonies, with some exceptions, and so its colonialism was arguably closer to what imperialism has become. Spanish men in Latin America, tellingly, were expected to get Indigenous or local brides. There was systemic anti-Black and anti-Indigenous racism throughout the Spanish Empire although the myth of a 'hybrid' ethnic identity remains strong, in Mexico and in Brazil especially. That means that there are similarities between the colonialism of the Spanish Empire and that of the French, British and Dutch empires.

But the Spanish Empire, in part due to its timing (starting with Columbus' arrival in the Caribbean in 1492), lacked both the domestic surplus population – not many Spanish peasants were keen to move to the Americas – and the bureaucratic wherewithal that would have been needed to successfully run colonies across the Atlantic.

After the emergence of independent Spanish-speaking republics in South America in the 1820s, Spain was arguably more imperialist than colonialist; but apart from a few ventures in North Africa its imperialist capacity was limited. It lacked a powerful army and especially navy, and there was no domestic bureaucracy like that in the Board of Trade and the India Office.

Like many current-day and nineteenth-century imperialist ventures, the Spanish Crown appropriated the colonies' resources, especially gold and silver. But Spain was a hopeless failure as an imperialist power. While the British became wealthy as a nation by the wholesale importation of codfish, beaver

25 See Bernard S. Cohn's analysis of the spectacle produced for the coronation of Queen Victoria as Empress of India, by in T. Ranger and E. Hobsbawm, eds., *The Invention of Tradition* (Cambridge, Cambridge University Press, 1976; second edition 2014).

26 There are no full-length critical studies of the JCPC even though it was important for this chapter because it was the court of final appeal for civil cases (including constitutional cases) for the British Empire from 1833 onward. But see the insider account by RB Haldane, himself a judge on the JCPC and an ex-Lord Chancellor, 'The Work for Empire [sic] of the Judicial Committee of the Privy Council', *Cambridge Law Journal* no. 1 (1922).

furs, spices, and plantation-made sugar, the silver and gold being mined by Indigenous people and/or African slaves in Latin America was not destined to stay in Madrid. It arrived in the southern Spanish port of Sevilla but quickly went into the coffers of the European banks (in the Low Countries and in the Italian city-republics) that saw the Spanish Crown as a great creditor/customer.

In the present day, virtually all Latin American countries are largely within the US sphere of influence, due to American financial, political and cultural domination. And today as in the past, the cultural is by no means unimportant. Hollywood, Disney and Amazon are major vehicles of US imperialism, not just Goldman Sachs and the New York Stock Exchange.

Conclusion

It is not easy, and may be unadvisable, to draw a sharp line separating empires from nation-states. As mentioned above, some contemporary geopolitical moves by both Russia and China suggest that some empires most people had thought were dead and buried may be re-emerging, though of course the new version of Empire, if it materializes, will not be identical to past forms.

But this chapter has eschewed sharp definitions, the kind of definitions, arranged in a classification, that are beloved of most sociologists including historical sociologists. Instead, it has mainly sought to clarify the meaning and significance of 'imperialism' (an economic, political, and sometimes military exercise of power) and the related but distinct 'colonialism'.

And while considering history, especially the history of Europe and its many settler and non-settler colonies turned independent states, the chapter has also touched on contemporary situations that can be helpfully analyzed by means of those two terms (imperialism and colonialism). Empire is indeed one of the key scales of political authority that is available for today's actors (especially those that enjoy a strong military apparatus and considerable economic influence).

While the overtly colonial and racist discourses found throughout the nineteenth and early twentieth centuries may suggest that empires and their cultural baggage including law are in the past, the example of contemporary American imperialism –exercised now not only by state actors alone but also by private companies from Elon Musk's 30,000 low-orbit satellites owned by Starlink to Walt Disney productions tell us that understanding the legal infrastructure of imperial power remains important today.[27]

27 Within legal studies, the large literature huddling under the acronym TWAIL (Third-World Approaches to International Law) has been largely concerned with the consequences of colonialism and the difficulties encountered by states seeking to become truly independent and post-colonial. This literature, at its height perhaps 20 years ago, has grown large enough that no one journal or publisher monopolizes it. Post-colonial and/or anti-colonial and anti-imperialist intellectual projects are too numerous to mention here, and can be found across a wide variety of journals, including legal history journals, socio-legal studies journals and history journals, and many social science journals.

2 The Scale of the Nation-State

In the first substantive chapter, Chapter 1, we mentioned that in the course of Foucault's account of the rise of modern states in Europe and the modes of power/knowledge that are found in different eras, he contrasts the unitary and centralizing logic of Empire to the logic of modern nation-states, which were born plural (see the Treaty of Westphalia for historical details).

The Sovereignty of Nation-States

This is more than a historical fact. It has great relevance today. Among other things, the fact that nation-states were born plural is relevant, indeed necessary, to understanding what the United Nations is and what it is not or what it cannot be.

People in law schools and out of them often complain that international law (made up mainly of UN conventions and treaties) has no enforcement agency, no 'world police' that can respond to violations of human rights or violations of other states' sovereignty. That is the case because state sovereignty is the key principle of the UN (and of its predecessor the League of Nations). If states are deemed equally sovereign then only voluntary action in the shape of peacekeeping troops can be expected of them in a major crisis (such as famine or civil war). If states are all sovereign regardless of conduct, aggressive or neo-colonial states (Putin's Russia comes to mind) also have to have their own sovereignty protected.[1]

The doctrine of state sovereignty is the main reason for the non-existence of a world police, even in an age where numerous 'humanitarian disasters' (as they are euphemistically called) exist. By and large, these so-called humanitarian disasters are the predictable result of either wars between states or of civil wars within states. A civil war can take place if one part of the state

1 Russia additionally benefits from being able to veto UN actions through their permanent membership in the UN Security Council. The UN Security Council was originally made up of the nations that won World War II, but there are non-permanent members elected by UN nation-states as well, although they do not enjoy the veto power that the permanent members have.

DOI: 10.4324/9781003612551-3

or one group seeking state power or trying to hold on to it goes to war with another part, as if it were a different country. Civil wars in African countries have often resulted in major 'humanitarian' crises. But the prevalence of civil wars and major civil conflicts (today's Haiti comes to mind) does not mean that old-fashioned wars between states are a thing of the past. The current invasion and bombing of Gaza by the Israeli state is a great example of a war that is arguably international (although Palestine is not recognized by the UN as a state, a problem that some European countries are attempting to remedy). If Palestine were a recognized state, then it would be easier for other countries and for the UN to denounce invasions and attacks. The statelessness of Palestinians as a group is an ongoing problem that casts rather a shadow on UN proceedings.

What is called a civil war or a civil armed conflict may well feature a totalitarian[2] government wreaking havoc on an undesirable domestic group, as happened in Syria under the Assad regimes, or as was the case in Saddam Hussein's Iraq. The so-called 'international' community, which as just mentioned cannot properly be described as a community despite the repetition of the phrase, cannot do much. States usually let international NGOs such as Medicins Sans Frontieres, the Red Cross and the Red Crescent tend to the sick and wounded.[3] And food for the starving is left to UN agencies as well as NGOs.

Why is there such a failure of real action? The reason is precisely that nation-states are, legally and politically, sovereign and independent entities. If a tyrant attacks his own people, the so-called international system cannot do much other than wring its collective hands. Currently, the attacks by the Kremlin's forces in Ukraine and the attacks on Gaza by the Israeli armed forces cannot be easily challenged by other states, given the 'all states are equally sovereign' doctrine.

In such situations (which amount to war against a people that is not admitted to constitute its own legally recognized state), if another state intervenes, sending military airplanes or drones and attempting to eliminate the domestic

2 On totalitarianism see Hannah Arendt's 1951 influential book, *The Origins of Totalitarianism* (multiple editions).Totalitarianism is more thoroughgoing in terms of controlling internal dissent than mere authoritarianism, though the two terms are often conflated. Authoritarian regimes might well have elections and might make some space for dissent, for example in certain news media. Arendt's work focused on the Soviet Union, which she saw, in contrast to the views of much of the left at the time, as equivalent to Hitler's Nazi Germany. Unfortunately, Arendt's view that Soviet communism and Nazism are morally and politically equivalent fails to take into consideration the progressive elements of socialism. Arendt's views were very popular in the United States, her adopted country (she was a German Jew), in the 1950s and 1960s.

3 There is a large critical literature on contemporary humanitarianism. Two leading studies are Didier Fassin, *Humanitarian Reason: A Moral History of the Present* (Berkeley, University of California Press, 2011) and Fleur Johns, *#Help: Digital Humanitarianism* (Oxford University Press, 2023).

tyrant, perhaps in the name of 'humanitarianism', there are suspicions about what many might see as covertly or not so covertly imperialist. As I write these lines President Trump and President Putin are meeting in Saudi Arabia of all places to 'sort out' Ukraine, but Ukraine is not represented in these talks between superpowers. President Trump seems to want to befriend both Russia and other states traditionally considered as enemies or at least competitors. Smaller or less powerful states seem to be poised to be the victims of the new imperialism. Imperial powers used to divide up less powerful countries and peoples to suit their own interests (as in the Berlin 1885 conference that divided Africa into imperial domains). As explained in the first chapter, currently there seems be a revival of imperial moves and rationales. Sheer power (financial, cultural and so on) is what separates an imperial power from a regular smaller or less powerful country.

Interference by a third state, no matter how humanitarian, is seen as illegitimate. Indeed, in the present moment, even the UNRWA, the main UN body that has for decades provided basic services to Palestinians in and out of the diaspora, has been deemed illegitimate by the government of Israel and that of the United States. UNRWA is not staffed by citizens of any one country but Israel and the United States act as if it were.

It is likely that many UNRWA personnel in Gaza were sympathetic to Hamas – living in Gaza would not be likely to make one sympathetic to Israel – but nevertheless UNRWA is an aid agency, and it has the UN seal of approval (for what that is worth at this time).

Let us turn the clock back to the early 2000s. Under the banner of 'the war on terror', both Tony Blair's UK and George W Bush's US did intervene in Iraq and Afghanistan, giving rise to large anti-war demonstrations, especially in the UK. Postcolonial scholars and activists would say that this intervention was a great example of the white West's desire to protect brown people from their own tyrannical governments, a desire which may be 'humanitarian' but does not exclude an imperialist agenda.

What has become clear is that such an intervention by white metropolitan Western countries into the affairs of global South poorer countries with non-white populations cannot be easily severed from the overtly imperial past of the 'international community', or at least of certain leading members of that so-called community. And US intervention, in both Kuwait and Iraq, was seen by many Americans as a mere struggle to control the flow of Middle East oil.[4]

4 Timothy Mitchell, *Carbon Democracy: Political Power in the Age of Oil* (London, Verso, 2023) is an influential study that traces the socio-economic foundations of the coal-based Europe-based industrial economy, and then zeroes in on the oil-based economy of the mid and late twentieth century, in which the United States became the most powerful player. Mitchell is a historian of the Middle East, especially Egypt, and traces the relationships between the different sources of energy and political formations.

We can see in this example of the post-9/11 War on Terror that imperialism has not been totally abandoned in the present, even though the United Nations recognizes the smallest of Pacific Island states as full members, on a par with the UK, France and the United Sates. That recognition of small island states allows us to claim that we live in an age of sovereign nation-states. But of course economic and military realities are what they are.

Imperialism and colonialism are not the kind of power relation that can easily be said to be on the junkheap of history. Yes, nation-states and their territorial sovereignty constitute the formal basis of the 'international system'. But as is recognized in such formal bodies as the UN Security Council, which has the powerful nations that won World War II as its permanent members, nation-states may be formally equal – but just as is the case with citizens, some of whom have a lot of power and money whereas others are poor and marginalized, so too nation-states are not in fact equal. Formal equality among all nation-states that are recognized by the UN is the basic principle of the United Nations, even though everyone knows that some countries are a lot richer and more influential than others. It is thus important to recognize that even though nation-states constitute the political map of the world today, imperialism and colonialism have not been left totally behind.

What Is 'The State' Anyway?

For the past 100 or so years, most of the critical work on 'the state' has taken place within a largely Marxist framework. Often, an anti-racist or feminist perspective was combined with Marxist views. Franz Fanon, for example, an important French intellectual originally from Martinique, was and remains an inspiration for those nations of brown and Black people that emerged from colonial status in the 1950s and 1960s. His work remains essential to understanding the international arena.

Given the heavy weight of Marxist ideas in analyses of states and of 'the state', it might be appropriate to preface the description of modern states[5] with a brief explanation about what the Marxist terms 'capitalism' and 'bourgeois society' have meant, since they occur frequently in left-wing accounts of 'the state' but they are often taken for granted, as if everyone knew what the terms meant.

Capitalism (and incidentally, Marx was not the only or first person to identify this as the main economic system prevalent in the nineteenth-century

5 Following Foucault I prefer to talk about describing states and outlining moves made typically by state actors rather than imagine that I or anyone else is providing a 'theory of the state'. Indeed, in my view, the phrase 'the state' already suggests a theoretical object rather than an actually existing entity. And the actually existing states are quite varied, especially if one includes historical examples as well as contemporary ones.

Europe and its colonies) is one 'mode of production'. A mode of production – feudalism, capitalism or a future socialism – is a particular arrangement of classes, whereby one class (the ruling class) monopolizes what Marx called the 'means of production'. Under feudalism the main means of production was land: hence the dominance of the landed aristocracy in some not fully modernized and capitalistic countries, even to this day.

In the industrial capitalism of the mid-nineteenth century, which was Marx's main object of study, the main means of production was the factory. Today that is no longer the case in much of the metropolitan Western world. Factories making products for Western consumption are often in global South countries far removed from the real centres of economic power, although they are closely linked to the centres of power through a variety of links, such as contracting out.

Today it might be said to be those that control much of the flow of financial capital are the ruling class. A combination of finance and what is called 'tech' but is actually the digital world (technologies have existed since the Roman Empire) seems to be in the ascendant, with traditional blue-collar factory jobs having largely departed from the richer countries. But financial capitalism is still capitalism. Workers/employees sell their labour to those who own and control the means of financial production. What is crucial here is that for Marx and his followers, the ruling class is not composed of just rich people. There are capitalists who struggle or who go bankrupt, and there are of course many workers/employees who are well paid, even very well paid, for their labour.

The bourgeoisie[6] that gave its name to 'bourgeois society' (a phrase that does not have a consistent meaning among authors) was, for Marx himself, the industrial bourgeoisie, the owners of firms. Whether the bourgeoisie has now been transformed beyond recognition, by the emergence of a professional-managerial class of executives, well-paid lawyers and accountants, etc. is not a question that has to be answered here.

In general, since Karl Marx's foundational work, theorizing 'the state' in critical social science and legal circles has meant reflecting on the varying ways in which economic interests – the interest of capitalists, mainly[7] – drive government policy.

6 Originally the 'burghers' were merchants who lived in cities (the country was then seen as full of peasants) and took active part in its governance –with the German term 'Burg' meaning city. A great fictional study of merchant bourgeois family relations is Thomas Mann's 191? *Buddenbrooks*, set in northern Germany in the early twentieth century.

7 Feudalism, the mode of production immediately preceding capitalism in European history, was also characterized by the private ownership of the main means of production, which was then land. Privatization of 'the commons', a key element in the transition from feudalism to capitalism, took place over a long period, usually facilitated by the state. The transition from feudalism to capitalism was still in process when Karl Marx was writing.

But despite many variations in the Marxist theme, a key idea that became accepted by the left-wing thinkers of the 1960s and 1970s was that capitalism was in fact, 'in the last instance', the major factor. By contrast, the judiciary, the military and other facets of 'the state' could be best understood as managing, as Lenin famously put it, 'the common affairs of the bourgeoisie'. Capitalism relies on firms that compete with one another, of course, but there are many issues (e.g. the rate of capital gains tax) that require a common agent. The production of money, for instance, is something that cannot be left to the marketplace. It requires a state. Tariffs, for instance, are within the purview of 'the state' – politicians and civil servants – but capitalist economies have certain common priorities and needs in respect of international issues such as tariffs.

The same goes for the value, in the global financial market, of the domestic currency. The value of currency cannot be left to the free market. It requires a central bank that will undertake things such as devaluation of the currency (which stimulates exports) and sets the basic interest rate for inter-bank borrowing. 'The state' also has to manage contradictions between different class fractions (to borrow Italian communist intellectual Antonio Gramsci's useful term). In Canada, for example, the largely Western oil and gas industries benefit from certain trade and monetary policies, but the same policies negatively affect the industrial production plants of Quebec and Ontario. Major political parties, in the major 'advanced capitalist' economies, tend to represent not a single class fraction but rather a more or less loose coalition of different class fractions. In Canadian politics, for example, the federal Conservative party has tended to favour the Western provinces, which export oil and gas and lumber and paper to the United States; but the Conservatives by no means neglect the industries located in Quebec and Ontario (such as auto parts manufacturing). As British Black scholar Stuart Hall said long ago, the secret of a governing party's success (Hall was analyzing 'Thatcherism') is found in somehow keeping together class fractions whose economic interests are by no means the same.

The same goes for other countries. The US Democrats, for instance, do not represent a single industry or sector. When in power federally Democrats will tend to act on behalf of any domestic sector that is seen as needing help. (For example, temporary foreign workers can be brought in to prop up select enterprises, such as agriculture, which might otherwise wither away due to labour costs). That the state – meaning, the legislature, the executive, the judiciary and, in many countries, the military – acts to minimize conflicts between capitalist sectors and promote what the common interests of the capitalist class seems more than justified if one looks at government policy.

Of course, the specifics of the state differ a great deal from one country to another. Some capitalist countries have independent judiciaries and even independent constitutional courts; others do not. Most common-law jurisdictions are tied to what is called the 'Westminster' system of parliamentary supremacy (which is why there are no written constitutional rights in the UK). But some would say that the supremacy of Parliament has become more of a fiction than a reality, whether in Britain or in countries such as Canada and Australia.

Differences are often visible in commonly used legislative and political moves that typically bring about policy change. The single-jurisdiction power that the American electoral system grants to individual senators or Congresspeople, who engage in negotiations of the 'you scratch my back and I'll scratch yours' type when confronted with difficult budget priorities, is unusual internationally. 'Log rolling' is a term often used in the halls of Congress to refer to this transactional process. Some Western American states, for example, have vast armies of workers in military industries, and their political representatives are not shy about defending their interest – even though little is gained by workers in other sectors and/or in other states from increasing military budgets.

In most countries, however, sectors and industries are often already well organized internally, so there is not as much by way of last-minute lobbying and negotiating. In some countries (Germany in particular) there is a long tradition of business, labour and government working together for what is seen as the common good – usually, the prosperity of capitalism, which is widely regarded as synonymous with the prosperity of all.

Overall, then, it is difficult to generalize about 'the state'. 'The state' does include a lot more than government proper: Opposition politicians, judges and the hordes of bureaucrats who staff the countless agencies of modern states play varying state roles, depending on the situation and the country's political traditions. In many countries, the military is also a significant part of 'the state', such as in Chile, Colombia, Brazil and other Latin American countries. In modern-day Europe, by contrast, armed forces are firmly under the control of civilian politicians (ministers of defence). That perhaps makes the armed forces less integral to 'the state' – although when crises are seen to arise (major drugs smuggling, for example) military as well as police bodies can be given more authority and more scope, and may even be identified as the visible hand of 'the state'.

In recent years the spectre of 'terrorism' has certainly worked to buff the prestige of both police and armed forces, even in countries that were historically seen as allergic to the military ethos. And in some countries, especially China, 'the state' maintains a large body of employees devoted to keeping tabs on the digital doings of citizens. One could say that China has become the main example of a nation-state that polices its digital space and protects those who are at the top of 'the state' against dissidents, in such a way as to suggest that the territory that needs protection and the assertion of sovereignty is not just physical/geographic but is also digital. The combination of digital surveillance and military power perhaps makes China the leading example of the contemporary state, insofar as surveillance of citizens as well as migrants has become key to the way today's states exercise their legal powers. And great military power has traditionally distinguished the so-called 'great' powers from ordinary countries.

Thus, even though the doctrine of respect for state sovereignty might suggest that all countries (at least those recognized by the UN) are on a level playing field, the old differences between major, even imperial powers and ordinary countries still persists today. To that extent it is difficult if not impossible to draw a sharp line separating empires from nation-states.

But whether in a 'great' power or in an ordinary country, citizens confront not only state law and international law but also local or municipal law. Which is the subject of the next chapter.

3 The Scale of the Local or Municipal

Introduction

This chapter will be divided into three parts, after a brief introduction recounting the fundamental insights of what one might call the 'first wave' of legal geographers, social scientists and legal scholars who were often mainly urbanists. Writers such as Neil Smith and Don Mitchell pursued a largely Marxist analyses of local law – American city ordinances, especially – pointing out that the local ordinances that had by the 1990s largely replaced old-fashioned vagrancy statutes that had traditionally targeted beggars, sex workers and 'dissolute' characters ('the usual suspects', in police parlance) ended up targeting the same groups, although by means of different legal tools.

The legal tools that emerged to replace vagrancy statutes that had been deemed unconstitutional by civil-rights oriented courts, mostly in the 1970s, focused on space. Indeed, they often or even always governed 'the usual suspects' THROUGH space.[1] This was done by adopting new rules (whose legal precedent were often medieval rules about where and when farmers or other markets could take place), rules governing how certain public urban spaces could or could not be used. These rules were on their face neutral as to persons and groups. In practice, however, they targeted many of the same groups as had been targeted by vagrancy statutes. Old-style offences such as public drunkenness, offering sexual services for sale or begging on sidewalks came to be replaced by ordinances and by-laws that looked constitutional on their

1 It is a commonplace of Foucaultian governmentality studies to suggest that people and activities can be governed not so much directly but through space, time, through architecture or by other less direct and personal means. This is rooted in Foucault's fulsome analyses of the effects of spaces such as prisons, mental hospitals and leper colonies. Confinement in a particular indoor space on a semi-permanent basis was a relatively early tool to govern disorderly people spatially; by the 1970s, confinement had largely been abandoned, partly because it was very expensive. 'De-institutionalization' became the by-word for governing disorderly people, especially the mentally ill. In the UK there was much talk about 'care in the community'. However, in the absence of serious expenditures on outpatient mental health, that nice-sounding slogan became a euphemism for 'living in poverty' in run-down urban areas, in rooming houses or similar 'bottom of the market' housing.

DOI: 10.4324/9781003612551-4

face because they did not name and explicitly exclude any groups. Indeed, these new ordinances and by-laws (which among other things involved a shift from the scale of the criminal law to the scale of local or regional governance) had the effect of reproducing or heightening existing social exclusions.

Don Mitchell and Neil Smith famously dubbed this governing-people-through-space in the name of urban order 'revanchism'. 'Revanchism' was a term derived from the French 'revanche', or revenge. The term was meant to connect the new space-oriented local rules to or with the rise of what was beginning to be called 'inner-city gentrification' (or in the UK, 'white painting'). Neil Smith published a book that gathered some of these analyses, a book that turned him into a major figure in left-wing urban studies.[2]

It is now almost cliché, and is certainly not original, to point out that legal rules that appear neutral on their face might in reality target particular already disadvantaged groups. As the famous French saying goes, the law in all its majesty prohibits the rich as well as the poor from sleeping under bridges: but only the poor experience the need to occasionally or for an extended time sleep under city bridges. By now, well into the twenty-first century, the *de facto* exclusionary character of rules that in theory only govern the use by anyone of urban spaces is well understood. This effect has been studied the most intensively insofar as the rules negatively affect homeless people. (The vulnerability of sex workers to being caught in and by these local rules is far less studied and known, by contrast, at least outside of feminist and queer urban studies).

Since the exclusionary effect of rules that govern the use of public spaces in a facially neutral but practically unequal manner is now well understood by diverse urban activists as well as by scholars of the urban, in this chapter we will move on to consider three other types of legal mechanism. These mechanisms rely more on private law tools than in planning-law tools and logics. These mechanisms are commonly used in cities around the world, and they do have definite structural or systemic inequality effects. However, the 'revanchist' thesis does not stress the differences in legal tools. The new 'revanchist' rules, almost always municipal or 'provincial', both reproduce and are based on different social norms than the old-style vagrancy statutes, which often targeted male unemployment. Three such types of legal tools will be considered here, one in each of the following three parts of the chapter.

All three parts are designed to highlight the characteristic feature of local or municipal governance as distinct from the workings of law at other scales – which is, to put it simply, that the exception is the rule. Social exclusion is not unique to the local. The income tax code of almost every country is full of

2 Don Mitchell, 'The Annihilation of Space by Law: Roots and Implications of the Anti-Homeless Ordinances in the US' *Antipode* vol. 29 no. 3 (1997), 303–335. Neil Smith, *The New Urban Frontier: Revanchism and the Gentrifying City* (London, Routledge, 1996).

exceptions that favour the already wealthy, for instance, and income tax codes are national. But ruling by means of generous mechanisms for granting exceptions easily, mechanisms that can mediate and continually postpone addressing a large variety of the kind of internal conflicts that are inherent to local and especially urban life, is a distintly local-scale phenomenon, I argue,[3] which draws the attention of researchers to the importance of scale in legal contexts.

Other scales of legal governance often contain and indeed are empowered or fuelled by exceptions made for certain individuals or groups. Income tax fraud, notoriously, is not as heavily policed or punished as many other arguably more minor frauds upon the state, to give but one example. (Comparing the fate of those who cheat on income tax with those charged with cheating by drawing 'too much' welfare reveals systemic injustices). Similarly, imperial law was often differentiated not only by colony or country but also by other lines drawn on the imperial map: lines drawing distinctions by religion, gender or ethnicity (often meaning ethnic differences as perceived or invented by the colonizers).

And yet, the fundamental logic of both national and imperial governing projects is one of expansionism and homogenization, as developed in the first chapter. That there is a single law for both rich and poor, for any and all religions, and so on is a founding myth of both modern nation-formation (with its central myth of 'the rule of law', with its corollary of 'equality before the law') and of the British Empire in particular. The British Empire constantly compared itself favourably to previous empires, and prided itself on disseminating 'British justice' everywhere, without much attention to local mores or local socio-economic distinctions. British justice was regarded as essentially and inherently superior, in keeping with the evolutionist paradigm that had Western Europeans at the climax of civilization.

By contrast, local governance in common-law jurisdictions is designed to provide ample opportunities for exceptions and exemptions. One situation that proves this point is the story of how it, despite the vocal opposition of private property owners and their allies in legislatures and the judiciary, the first successful zoning ordinance in the United States was the 1916 zoning ordinance meant to regulate the height and bulk of Manhattan skyscrapers but not coincidentally also relegating factories (and their workers, who apparently disturbed upper-class shoppers) into areas of the city not previously set aside for respectable residential uses.[4] The fact that local/municipal law in the

3 For more on the distinctive character of local law see Mariana Valverde, 'Urban Legal Forms and Practices of Citizenship' in A. Amin and M. Lancione., eds. *Grammars of the Urban Ground* (Durham NC, Duke University Press, 2022), 108–125.

4 See Keith Revell, *Building Gotham: Civic Culture and Public Policy in New York City, 1898–1938* (Baltimore NJ, Johns Hopkins University press, 2003). Revell shows that the 1916 ordinance that was then copied or imitated in many cities was successful precisely because a local legal mechanism existed to provide generous exceptions. Without the exceptions mechanism

United States contains the curious term 'legal nonconforming' is of interest here.

In other areas of law one cannot exempt certain places or people from, say, the criminal law on theft; but in planning law, land uses that no longer conform to a new plan or zoning ordinance can be 'grandfathered' as what in North America is called 'legal nonconforming uses'. A mechanic's garage that has long operated (perhaps under different ownerships) in a residential street can, for example, be labelled as 'legal nonconforming' and allowed to continue operating, without the overall residential zoning of the street coming into question.[5] I argue that the category of 'legal nonconforming' and its equivalents in various common-law jurisdictions tells us something very important about the structure of *local* law and governance.

Local/municipal law can also be said to be more pragmatic and less principle-based than other areas of law (not unrelated to the exception-as-the-rule notion just described). Constitutional law is notoriously principle-driven. This means that challenges to the constitutionality of, say, a certain police action will be decided by precedents that are usually principle-based. 'The rule of law', 'equality before the law', freedom of speech, freedom of association and other such principles are the bread and butter of constitutional law.

Municipal actions, by contrast, can problem-solve in a pragmatic kind of way rather than by the top-down application of grand principles that is the essence of constitutional law. Garbage collection and pothole filling, to name two everyday examples of local legal action, are not well suited to grand principles. A city manager can simply propose that X works better than Y as a method of trash collection, and that purely pragmatic decision can be considered legally valid if confirmed by the elected councillors, which often is no more than a rubber stamping exercise.

Hence, to connect the two points just made: municipal or local law is both more shot through with exceptions (with exemptions from rules being relatively easy to get) and is more pragmatic than 'higher' levels of law.[6] That makes local law in practice more akin to mediation than to law enforcement.

(known variously as rulings by a board of appeals or a committee of adjustment), the ordinance would likely have been repealed by courts and/or legislatures. This looming threat of invalidation by courts or legislatures was due to the fact that zoning greatly interferes with the rights associated with private property ownership. In the United States as in many other countries, private property rights are embedded in the constitution itself.

5 For evidence on this point from Toronto, see Mariana Valverde, *Everyday Law on the Street: City Governance in an Age of Diversity (*Chicago, University of Chicago Press, 2012).

6 The form of power exercised by municipalities through bylaws and ordinances deploys a particular kind of knowledge, an experience-based reasoning that often sets aside the letter of the law. I saw this when I was doing an empirical study of municipal inspectors and was told by an official that the 'fence viewers' whose job was to mediate disputes between neighbours about fences did not see their job as enforcing any general rules, but simply reaching a compromise that both neighbours could live with. For a more theoretical and historical elaboration of this point,

That does not mean that grand principles (such as equality before the law) do not play a role but they play a role too in virtually every other area or scale of law. What is distinctive about local governance is the prevalence and legal acceptability of 'what works' as opposed to the battles of principles that appeal courts often adjudicate. (For instance, freedom of religion as opposed to gender equality, where both are grand principles but both cannot be simultaneously accomodated). The area of law in which one can best see this pragmatic approach is nuisance law. Nuisance lawsuits are rare today: they have been largely replaced by the enforcement of codes and rules (including zoning). Nevertheless the logic of nuisance persists, municipally or locally. Nuisance has always been site-specific and even person-specific, since what is bothersome to one type of person is not considered as universally bothersome, and if there is nobody to be bothered nuisance does not exist.[7]

The section that immediately follows this introduction tackles the question of 'what is the dividing line between law and non-law in local governance?' It will argue that while municipal jurisdiction to pass laws is highly limited in many respects by legislatures, courts and 'higher' levels of government (e.g. states, in India or the United States), there are numerous regulatory systems that while falling outside the strict letter of the law (they are not embedded in ordinances or by-laws) function as law, and in some cases have more power than law, in that it is physically or legally impossible to depart from the rules. Technical standards are the best example of such regulations, which are not exactly law because they are not legislated by city councils or other local-scale legislative bodies, such as county councils or township councils.

The second part is based on the growing literature on contractually based local communities. From a legal perspective this section highlights not so much legislative pronouncements or even technical standards, but rather contracts. Gated communities are the best example here, but as we will see there are many types of contractually based local bodies. The climate catastrophe is bringing out conflicts between and within localities that were smoothed over in the past or subject to technocratic governance. As we shall see contractually based local communities, in practice, challenge the longstanding liberal myth about the consent of the governed and the free will of the contractual parties.

---

based on the history of nuisance law, see Mariana Valverde, 'Seeing Like a City: The Dialectic of Modern and Premodern Modes of Knowledge in Local Governance' *Law and Society Review* vol. 45 no. 2, 277–312 (2011).

7 An interesting factoid about English nuisance law is that the monarch can never be considered as a nuisance, even during royal visits to private spaces. See Davina Cooper, 'Far Beyond "the Early Morning Crowing of a Farmyard Cock": Revisiting the Place of Nuisance in Legal and Political Discourse' *Social and Legal Studies* vol. 11, no. 1 (2003), 5–35. Among other things, Cooper points out that the English law of nuisance fails to control the invasion of privacy caused by royal visits to hospitals and homes: the Crown cannot, by definition, cause a nuisance.

Finally, the third part will tackle a topic that has not been much explored in the urban studies literature: the existence and possible rapid growth of what one could call 'urban legal islands'. There are many urban spaces where the by-laws and ordinances of the relevant city council do not apply. A few examples of urban legal islands will be briefly discussed, with the aim of stimulating discussion, in university classes or in the public arena, of the significance of these 'special' spaces.

All in all, the three sections are designed to challenge the myth that a city is a homogenous space that is essentially a mini-state. I argue that there is a qualitative difference between realms such as constitutional law and criminal law, on the one hand, and local/municipal law on the other. The difference may be more of degree than of kind, since principles are by no means absent in local governance (especially when cities take on principle-based campaigns, such as being a 'sanctuary city'). And vice versa: forms of pragmatic governance are not completely foreign to 'higher' levels of government. But for purposes of legal geography, we have to pay attention to commonly found differences between scales of governance. It is therefore important to make a few generalizations about what is 'typical' or special about local/municipal law. Cities, to name the most common example of local governance, are simply not mini-territories that demand homogeneity in legal governance. For this very reason, cities are not sovereign entities, and as a result cannot build walls to keep out migrants from the countryside. As the medieval saying went, 'city air makes one free' – because serfs became free if they managed to survive within a city for one year. Cities do not enjoy legal sovereignty. In Canadian law, for instance, cities are not 'the Crown', whereas there are ten (or twelve) provincial Crowns, and one federal Crown that is dispersed among ministries and agencies. The 'petty' disputes that plague city solicitors and other lawyers working at the municipal scale include both disputes between neighbours and conflicts between citizens and the city apparatus. I once interviewed a city official who said that the problem that occupied more of his time than any other was inter-family disputes about dogs in parks. At that time I thought 'how mundane'. But soon I decided that mundane disputes were indeed important, if I was going to understand how 'the city' (meaning both the formal civil service and the larger socio-economic entity also called 'the city') worked or didn't work but persisted. These days, being a professor emeritus, I am not often on campus, but I am more or less available for media calls.

I make fun of my own expertise by saying that I get calls from journalists asking if it is true that children running lemonade stands on sidewalks are committing an illegal act. To that query I respond, 'yes it is true that it's against the vending bylaw', but I then add that no municipal inspector would think of fining the kids or their parents. They know how 'the law in the books' does not coincide with 'the law in practice' – the founding principle of socio-legal studies.

The Boundaries of 'Law' and the Importance of Technical Standards

To start with a personal experience anecdote. Travelling to southern Chile in 2018, I discovered that my hotel had two types of electrical sockets, at the same time, often in the same room. One type of socket was designed in the same way as the European continental plug used in France, Spain and Italy. The other was the North American socket used in the United States and Canada. Being curious about infrastructure, I asked my hosts about the two-plug problem. They told me that southern Chile was regarded as a remote market by the big electricity companies that were busy signing deals with governments throughout Latin America. Therefore, a French company had a contract for electricity in many places (including the town where I was, Temuco) but an American company also had a contract for the same locations. That was the cause of the two-socket system.

Of course the situation was favourable for travellers like me, with a limited capacity to convert from one system of electrical outlets to another. In every space I went in the southern Chile town of Temuco, I could find an American-style outlet and plug in my bought-in-Canada laptop. But I could also have used the French style, which was familiar to me because it is the same as what is used in Spain. Incidentally, the 'continental' outlet differs significantly from the one prevalent in Britain: it has two prongs, not three. I realized that my siblings in Barcelona would have enjoyed travelling to a place in which they could use their laptops and other gadgets without any converter.

The situation that I am calling the two-plug problem highlights the importance of what are called technical standards in shaping our experience of urban space. People who travel internationally are used to carrying with them one of those multi-socket gadgets that one can buy at airports. Perhaps they don't notice that the technical standards set out by whichever electricity company operates in a certain area have more than the force of law. Laws after all can be resisted, ignored or broken. But there is no equivalent of breaking the law in the world of technical standards.

I argue that if legal scholars are intent on capturing law 'in practice', and not just 'law in the books', technical standards need to be included in the study. Each city, and indeed each locality, rural or urban, has a whole host of standard-driven coercions. I say 'coercion' because the technical world acts coercively on us, even though we don't see the coercion at work. Trying to insert a plug for a shaver or a laptop into the 'wrong' outlet is totally futile. Resistance is futile, as they say.

The important role of technical standards in local governance – or national governance for that matter, since many industry-specific standards are national – can be illustrated by going over, say, an ordinary house and its contents. Baby clothes are often forced by the law of standards to be fire-resistant, or they will not be offered for legal sale. Telephones have countless technical standards, which may be designed to facilitate cross-national conversations while retaining a flavour of the local (as in the British two-tone ring that even Android or Iphone cell phones have).

Importantly for law, engineers, not legislators, usually decide on standards for such important things as the width and depth, and length of the numerous utility cables that lurk under city streets. Engineers or other private sector personnel also decide the amount of space and the quantity of dirt that sidewalk trees can (and must) enjoy. And so on. The building code, an aggregation of technical standards, is in each jurisdiction stronger than law. Once more, resistance is futile. Some resistance is possible, but not much.

An example of the powerful force of 'technical' standards consists of the rules about underground utility cables and pipes. One engineer reportedly told a researcher, a PhD student I knew, that it would be far better for 'the city' (meaning, in his case, the municipal civil service) if the roots of trees could be persuaded to grow in straight lines. As it is, tree roots often interfere with fibre optic and other cables under the sidewalk. Tree roots and other natural entities cannot be dictated to by technical standards. Citizens can, however.

While many urban studies and criminological scholars study the exclusionary effects of certain city council-backed by-laws and ordinances, formal law, that is by-laws or ordinances, are just the tip of the iceberg.

Regulations about what park benches ought to look like and what they cannot look like are not likely to be embedded in by-laws; they are far more likely to originate either in the industry that makes outdoor furniture or in jurisdiction-specific technical standards drawn up mainly by engineers.[8] Few city councillors, aldermen or township- and county-level authorities would claim that their authority has been usurped by the engineering profession. But a critical analysis of actual local governance might well show that visible legislative activity is only the tip of the iceberg. How street lights are distributed, how traffic lights are installed or not installed are matters usually deemed as 'technical', not legal. But the example of my trip to Chile at the start of this section perhaps calls that sense of the boundaries of law into question. It's not that technical standards are law; they are not. But they have more than the force of law, and implementing technical standards is regarded as less political and less controversial than implementing new by-laws. Norms can be more successfully embedded in standards than in laws.

A thorough study of local governance would thus not stop with the legislative activity of the local body in question (a city council, a county council,

8 For the regulation of sidewalk spaces and activities by engineers, see Nicholas Blomley, *Rights of Passage: Sidewalks and the Regulation of Public Flow* (London, Routledge, 2013). Technical standards often conceal a social or economic rationale, and they either help or hinder environmental efforts. That is the case for the standards decided by engineers and implemented by the urban forestry department for sidewalk trees.

etc.) Such a study would include the realm of the 'technical'. The technical exercises are largely taken for granted. Scholars in Science and Technology Studies (STS) often document just those 'standards' that act to govern conduct more successfully than law. To this end, anthropological work on infrastructure is particularly important, and could be read by legal scholars with much profit.[9]

Socio-legal studies, especially in the United States, are often undertaken through an unspoken sociological paradigm. In that frame, conscious action by individuals and groups is privileged, as is formal law. The term 'agency' is constantly bandied about as that which ought to be documented, now that a focus on structures has come to be seen as Marxist and therefore old-fashioned. But what are called technical standards are in a way more than law, higher than law: they cannot be defied.But technical standards embedded in everything from walls and paints to baby clothes are also 'under' the law, infra-legal so to speak, because no legislative body has passed them or even discussed them.

Contract-Based Local Communities

There is a vast literature on gated communities, which among other things show that not all gated communities are private property. Some more or less gated communities are occupying public streets (although some I saw in Mexico City a few years ago were actually on public streets, but had somehow managed to instal physical barriers to separate them from the general city, a move that was likely technically illegal but was tolerated by all. The neighbors living in this enclave had somehow found a way to together pay private security personnel to staff the non-legal but socially accepted barriers).[10]

A commonly found contract-based community is a building or a development with several buildings that is legally organized as a condominium. The condominium is a form of housing tenure and property whereby each family or unit holds their own unit in purely private ownership, fee simple in the UK, and holds the common property (garden, elevators, common spaces such as party rooms) in common. When someone leaves the condominium and sell their unit, the relevant share of the jointly owned common property goes with

9 See Kregg Hetherington, ed., *Infrastructure, Environment and Life in the Anthropocene* (Chapel Hill, Duke University Press, 2019).

10 An influential study of gated communities in Latin America, where paying for private security mechanisms is often regarded by well-off households as an effective anti-crime measure, is Teresa Caldeira, *City of Walls: Crime, Segregation and Citizenship in Sao Paulo* (Berkeley, University of California Press 2000). Gated communities are very popular in Argentina and Colombia as well as in Brazil. Needless to say the gated community is built on the assumption that crime always threatens from the outside: domestic violence, incest and child abuse are thus made invisible. Much of the literature on gated communities neglects this patriarchal aspect.

the apartment or house. For a long time, condominium ownership was not available in common-law jurisdictions due to the common law's fixation with land. As Doug Harris has shown for Vancouver, which in Canada invented the condo, lawyers in that jurisdiction (British Columbia) had to mobilize the already fantastical notion of 'air rights' (property rights to the air above a real estate property) in order to construct a new form of property law, the condominium.[11] Bourgeois families in Paris and Barcelona had owned their apartments for many decades. But in the common-law world, the emergence of the condominium was slowed by the common law's fixation on owning not just a building but also, and especially, the land underneath it. This fixation (based on a long history of largely rural properties) is somewhat at odds with the common-law doctrine that the Crown ultimately owns all the land, but various legal fictions have been devised to get around that contradiction. Eventually inventive lawyers made sure that even if condo owners did not own the land beneath their building, they could rightfully own their units.

The considerable US literature on 'special district governments' (which are said to be more numerous than incorporated municipalities, with the exact number unknown since the Census does not record them)[12] suggests that in the United States, especially in the Southwest, many contractual communities were and still are not all-purpose gated communities but rather supra-municipal utilities 'special purpose' governments, such as districts or fire protection bodies. One can currently see, in California and other Western states, fire districts in which a county-based fire service or even a state-created body is contracted to provide services to some municipalities.

In the US West, the current environmental crisis in the Colorado River is likely to put pressure on the traditionally quiet, technocratic management of the Southern California Water District, which not surprisingly is the largest such entity in the state. Los Angeles does have a separate entity to manage its drinking water supply, as is the case in most large cities: but the typical inhabitant of LA is unlikely to know that the Los Angeles Department of Water and Power imports nearly a third of its water from the distant Owens Valley, known by the indigenous Paiute people as Payahuunadü, 'The Land of the Flowing Water'.

It is likely that as the Colorado River is affected negatively by climate change, and is tapped by an increasing number of residential districts in the

11 Doug Harris, 'The Condominium: Transformations in Property Law and Local Governance' in the *Routledge Handbook of Property, Law and Society* (London, Routledge, 2023), Chapter 9.

12 The United States has countless 'special district governments' – arguably made necessary by the weakness and tiny territorial reach of most incorporated municipalities. These can include water districts, fire districts and police districts, operating at a supra-municipal scale. But contractualism is visible in state governance as well. See inter alia Jody Freeman, 'The Contracting State' *Florida State University Law Review* (2000-1), at p. 155, and Jody Freeman and Martha Minow, eds., *Government by Contract* (Cambridge MA, Harvard University Press, 2009).

US Southwest, including in Nevada, conflicts between municipalities, and between municipalities and supra-municipal 'water districts', will increase.[13] There is nothing like drought to stimulate social and economic conflicts.

The point here is that the extreme proliferation of incorporated municipalities in the United States, especially the West, causes governance deficiencies when events such as environmental disasters and droughts take place. Which entity is tasked with issuing water restrictions, for instance, is not obvious in the case of supra-municipal water districts serving many incorporated municipalities and also non-incorporated rural areas, private gated communities, and other types of local entity. LA County, for example, has 88 incorporated municipalities (some as small as 'West Hollywood' which according to the 2020 US Census had just over 35,000 inhabitants) and in addition some unincorporated rural areas.

Such a legal structure works mainly to serve the interests of ratepayers in high-income municipalities, who, lacking a metropolitan level of government, are not obligated to contribute to fund schools or police services in lower-income areas. The role of micro-municipal government in increasing inequality (across large metropolitan areas, such as LA) has been amply shown in relevant socio-legal scholarship.[14]

Overall, then, the absence of metropolitan-scale elected authorities that could institute some level of legal redistribution is a major problem in the face of increasing social and economic inequality. Some cities do have a metropolitan level of government (New York in the United States, Manchester in the UK) but many do not.

One insight from legal geography that can help those trying to understand phenomena such as American municipal fragmentation and the rise of privatized contractual communities (whether they have a gate or not, and whether that gate is legal or not, as in my Mexico city example) is that economic inequality is closely connected to spatial inequality.

Spatial inequality, visible in the legal fragmentation of municipal incorporation in the United States, can act to increase existing inequalities. One can see this in almost every city in the world. Cities around the world are not homogenous spaces. Areas deemed 'good' neighbourhoods not only enjoy

13 The Colorado river is currently drying up, due both to increased demand for water and to climate-related factors. This will affect not only drinking water supplies (and American family habits such as watering grass-centric lawns, washing cars with potable water, and taking daily showers) but also electricity production. See Robert Adler, *Law and the Colorado River* (Salt Lake City, University of Utah Press, 2024). See also the two 'water conflicts' articles in Mariana Valverde et al, eds., *Routledge Handbook of Law and Society* (London, Routledge, 2020).

14 An influential study of the curious fragmentation of American local democracy is Gerald Frug *Building Communities Without Building Walls* (Princeton University Press, 2009). See also Yishai Blank, *The City and the World* (free paper on SSRN and academia.edu, https://www.academia.edu/20887772/The_City_and_the_World

better privately owned housing and upscale retail businesses but also have better access to green space and even to public transit.

Spatial inequality is perhaps another word for the divide between 'good' and 'bad' neighbourhoods that almost every city in the world features, and which can readily be seen through one's own eyes. 'Good' neighbourhoods have more valuable private property, both commercial and residential: but they also have better public spaces – more green areas, more trees, more playgrounds and fancier avenues and boulevards with interesting public art. They also usually have less crime than 'bad' neighbourhoods.

Spatial inequality is one of the key concepts that legal geography has offered the world. It is a useful idea for all social sciences. Demographic and income data do not suffice to document the everyday experiences of living in a locality. Spatial inequality can be seen with one's own eyes as one traverses a local space, especially an urban, highly differentiated space. It includes perceptions, cultural tropes (e.g. 'common knowledge' ideas about the presence or absence of 'gangs') and culturally shared feelings. If single women do not feel safe walking down a particular street, it is useful to ask why those feelings exist and why they are likely to be shared by many women (though not all, since feelings of safety and danger are highly racialized as well as gendered).[15]

Urban Legal Islands

The third and final part of this article will also stray from urban legal geography's focus on the exclusionary effects of all-purpose general ordinances or by-laws. The reason for the neglect of exceptionality in local law is that we have for over 30 years now had studies of the socio-economic exclusionary and often also racist effects of general-purpose by-laws or ordinances passed by city councils or other legislative bodies. For example, American city ordinances that ban lying in the doorways of commercial establishments target the people who are likely to be tired due to not having a bed to sleep in. These 'street people' are not a representative sample of the population but are those people who were formerly governed coercively through 'vagrancy' laws.

Many studies have also shown that contemporary cities do not just use by-laws and ordinances; they use physical measures. (This is where the force of technical standards coincides with the force of other inequalities enshrined in law). Park benches began to be designed so one could not sleep on them. Flowerbed edges and other public surfaces had obstacles inserted into concrete in order to prevent skateboarding. What the industry of 'Crime

15 There are numerous studies of spatial inequality undertaken by urban geographers and others. Many document gender-specific experiences. An interesting one based on the experiences of LGBTQ people in urban settings is Les Moran and Bev Skeggs, *Sexuality and the Politics of Violence and Safety* (London, Routledge 2004).

Prevention Through Environmental Design' called 'defensive architecture' spread from one city to another.

But not all urban space is covered by a single urban or municipal legal system. Space, especially urban space, is highly differentiated. Even medieval cities had 'good' and 'bad' neighbourhoods. This differentiation is sometimes legal. There are in contemporary cities all manner of spaces where the casual observer might imagine that bylaws and ordinances of general application apply, but that would be wrong. Many spaces are legally unique, or without being visibly unique are removed from by-laws of general application passed by democratic bodies such as city councils. They are what I and my friend Alex Flynn (law professor at the University of British Columbia) call 'urban legal islands'.

Urban legal islands are more numerous now than they used to be, but they are not new. They are not the invention of neoliberalism, as some scholars might want to claim. A good example of an urban legal island that is much older than neoliberalism is the space known world-wide as Central Park, in New York City. That famous park, featured in countless Hollywood movies and TV series and hence familiar virtually everywhere, is governed by the city's park by-laws to some extent. But it also has its own system of what one can only call private governance. It turns out, when one looks beneath the surface, that the park (perhaps the most famous park in the world) is a legal island. It is run not by the city parks department but rather by an entity known as the Central Park Conservancy, whose website does not give its date of foundation but states it has a 40-year history.

In a good number of cities, in many common-law jurisdictions, some parks (usually the ones that draw tourists or are in some way 'special') are not regular city parks under the jurisdiction of the Parks department. In the United States, many parks were organized, legally, as an public-private partnership, from the late nineteenth century onwards. The boards of the Conservancies (and public library boards too, sometimes) were generally dominated by the local elites, or in some cases the wives of the local elite businessmen. These 'ladies who lunch' would have been called 'philanthropists' even if they did not give a single cent to charities supporting the city's poor. Being on the board of a park Conservancy (or a library board, in the case of those cities that had semi-private library boards) adds to the social capital of the men and women on the board, and the social capital of their families as well.

A key feature of the decision to set up a separate, volunteer parks board for a certain park was that fundraising could target just that park, not the city parks department. Today, the global moneyed elites living around Central Park can donate to the Central Park Conservancy and know that their money is being used for improvements in that particular park –not put into the general budget of the parks department. No doubt there are many public spaces including parks in underprivileged areas of the city that could use more basketball courts or more green spaces: but the overall budget of the parks department is tied to the city's property tax base, which may not be as generous as the philanthropic donations of the elites living near Central Park.

It is a curious feature of US urban history that parks and some semi-public libraries (the most famous being the ones partially financed by Andrew Carnegie, who was always careful to ensure that the future upkeep of 'his' libraries was a city financial responsibility) often had their own boards. As is still the case in numerous institutions, the public purse was responsible for maintenance and upkeep and overhead costs, whereas the philantropic donation was a one-time gift.

The practice of letting the public entity bear the operating costs into the indefinite future, while the donation remains a one-time gift, is still today the main way to channel philanthropic donations to what one can call 'urban legal islands'. In Toronto, where I live, the best example of this kind of public-private partnership, responsible for what some urbanists would call a 'premium' space, is the Bentway, a special park recently built under a highway featuring an ice skating path that is very popular in the winter and a number of 'permitted' events in the good-weather months. People using the Bentway's facilities might imagine that 'the city' is the creator and maintainer of the space, but in fact that is not the case. It is not legally called a conservancy but its logic is the same as that of the Central Park Conservancy. A crucial point here is that philanthropic donations all too often go to public spaces that are already what critical urbanists call 'premium' spaces.[16] Giving a large donation to the parks department of a city so that public servants can allocate it to where there is the most need is not what upper-class philanthropists want to do with their surplus cash.

In addition to the 'premium' spaces favoured by upper-class philanthropists then and now, there are also a large number of urban legal islands created for very contingent, site-specific reasons. One example from Vancouver is Granville island, a premium tourist-oriented space. Granville island is not part of the city proper but is rather owned by and run by a technocratic federal authority, the Canadian Housing and Mortgage Corporation.

The greater Vancouver area is perhaps unusually rich in these extra-municipal entities. The main campus of the University of British Columbia, which had in its origins been designated a military reserve and was hence federal, is unusual internationally in that it is not within any municipality. When a development is contemplated, one aspect or branch of 'the university' gives permission to proceed to the development/real estate side.)

16 The one-sided participation of philanthropists in the construction and maintenance of public spaces, indoor and outdoor, is also visible in the way in which donations to universities are channelled. Operating costs are almost never included in the donation. See Mariana Valverde et al, 'Public Universities as Real Estate Developers in the Age of the Art of the Deal' *Studies in Political Economy* vol 101, no. 1 pp. 35–58.

In addition to these one-off, legally unique entities that are not marked off by fences but are legally islands within the city –or legal islands outside the city proper, such as the main campus of the University of British Columbia – there are specific by-laws for particular spaces. There are many public parks that have their own set of by-laws. In England, the rules governing specific parks are often helpfully posted on prominent signs at the entrance. The lists are mainly 'don'ts' – don't play football, don't drink alcohol, and so on. The special spaces may also come in the shape not of a park or a small set of libraries but rather a distinct urban district. The latter are more difficult to discern than park conservancies because there is seldom a physical marker of legal distinctiveness. But in the United States in particular, public-private partnerships designed to 'improve' or 'renew' a particular, bounded district, usually in the central business district, have existed and prospered since the late nineteenth century.[17] In New York City, the Port Authority[18] continues today to exempt itself from zoning and other general city rules, in respect of the important urban properties it holds (including the land where the twin towers once stood).

In Toronto, where I live, there are two main squares that are the obvious places to have a rally or demonstration. One is Nathan Phillips square (in front of city hall) and the other is Dundas Square (at Yonge and Dundas, the Canadian intersection with the highest pedestrian count). They both have site-specific by-laws and are therefore legal islands. Dundas square is not even really a public square, since it is governed by a mysterious faceless public-private partnership (see their website at yds.ca). The website of this conservancy-style entity declares that one needs permits from the police to call any kind of protest there. Not surprisingly the square is almost never used for demonstrations. Political protests are funnelled either into Nathan Phillips

17 The fragmentation of urban space, and indeed of 'the city' accomplished in this manner is a common phenomenon. In the UK there are 'regeneration' districts, and in the US 'urban improvement' or 'urban development' districts. More recently innovative financial tactics have combined to fragment urban governance and even urban space itself more thoroughly. See for example Rachel Weber, 'Selling City Futures: the Financialization of Urban Redevelopment Policy' *Economic Geography* vol. 86 no. 3, 251–274, and Stephanie Farmer, 'Cities as Risk Manageers: The Impact of Chicago's Parking Meter P3' *Environment and Planning A*, vol. 46, pp. 2160–2174.

For the UK the Thatcherite invention of the Private Finance Initiative was crucial. See Martin Loughlin, *Legality and Locality: The Role of Law in Central-Local Government Relations* (Oxford, Clarendon, 1996).

18 For an account that features legal inventiveness in the foreground, see Jameson Doig, *Empire on the Hudson: Entrepreneurial Vision and Political Authority in the New York Port Authority* (New York, Columbia University Press, 2001). For a more recent example of urban 'regeneration' that highlights legal conflicts between the city, the Port Authority and the private developer who unluckily bought the ninety-nine-year lease to the twin towers shortly before they were demolished, see Lynn Sagalyn, *Power at Ground Zero: Politics, Money and the Remaking of Lower Manhattan* (New York, Oxford, 2016).

square or, more frequently, on the front lawn of the provincial legislature at Queen's Park, where protesters are surrounded by many lanes of high-speed traffic.

Concluding Remarks

The three sections of this chapter have all highlighted two themes. One is the solid pragmatism of urban governance, including legal governance. By-laws are not always enforced even in theory, never mind in practice. Instead, compromises based on practical concerns are regarded as 'good' solutions to the conflicts that always haunt the local, especially the urban.

The second point made throughout the chapter is that cities are not mini-states. Urban law (often confused with municipal law, even by lawyers) is especially prone to being used to differentiate spaces legally rather than subsume spaces under a coherent set of legal rules. Urban legal islands are perhaps the most obvious example of urban space's legal differentiation. But urban legal islands, from gated communities to 'special' parks, are not only legal: they are also socially and politically and culturally constructed.

Critical urban studies' notion of 'premium' spaces is helpful: it highlights how public resources often end up channelled to the spaces that are already 'premium' by virtue of being seen as 'good' neighbourhoods. Private entities such as gated communities or condominium developments that are seen as 'good' or even 'best' end up having more flowers, more trees, and more park space than neighbourhoods that could arguably be in greater need of green space. That municipal greenery has a troubling tendency to follow the concentration of private money, rather than work towards spatial equity, is arguably the biggest problem in local governance today. To look at this issue in more detail, the next chapter is devoted to 'premium' spaces, and more generally to micro-local legal governance.

4 The Scale of the Micro-Local

This chapter will address the question that runs throughout the book, that is, how a particular scale of governance – in this case, local, not national, and not transnational or imperial – works differently from other scales used to see and to govern spaces, including urban spaces.

But it will do so not by focusing on 'the city' proper and its rules of general application (covered in the previous chapter) but rather on the current trend towards the scale of the micro-local. That scale is associated with and/or legally enabled by the privatization of certain select spaces within a municipality (especially urban ones).[1] I argue in this chapter that many urban spaces that look like public spaces are not all 'public' in the strict sense (being publicly owned and being open to any member of the public).

The chapter expands on work already done on how 'seeing like a neighbour' differs from 'seeing like a city' – but th focus is not so much on formally designated neighbourhoods, which are sometimes rather large, but rather on what I call 'urban legal islands'. Those are spaces that may look as if they are part of a homogenous city governed by a single set of rules, but are in fact, and in law, *sui generis* entities, often structured through what some call 'public-private partnerships'[2].

These urban legal islands have been studied in major global cities, mainly New York, where Zucotti park, the site of the Wall Street protests of 2008–2009, was brought to international attention due to the fact that it turned out that the so-called park, which looked as if it were public, was in fact a privately owned public space or what is known in urban planning as a POPS.

1 In general, cities are often divided, by popular consensus or through real estate marketing practices, into distinct neighbourhoods. Toronto, for example, has 140 neighbourhoods, as shown on the city's municipal maps. By contrast, rural municipalities can and do exist without much spatial differentiation. There can be 'micro-local' projects in rural municipalities, but such projects are rare. A rare geographer who did not confuse the local with the urban was the late British geographer Doreen Massey, author of *For Space* (London, Sage, 2005).

2 On public-private partnerships, which I argue are not one thing but a range of different arrangements, see chapter 5 of Mariana Valverde, *Infrastructure: New Trajectories in Law* (London, Routledge, 2022).

DOI: 10.4324/9781003612551-5

Therefore the private owner could and did 'evict' the protesters. Trespass laws are a private-law tool, most often used by private security guards posted at commercial buildings to boot out 'trespassers' such as unhoused people who are trying to sleep in doorways, bus shelters and the like.

If the protesters had gathered in an actually public space, such as a municipal park, they could not have been evicted; eviction is a power that private property owners monopolize. They would have had to be charged with municipal offenses such as setting up tents in parks or littering, offences that many police officers consider beneath their notice and/or their pay grade. Municipal inspectors are usually far less numerous than police officers, ten to one being a not unusual ratio. Municipal officers do not have powers of arrest: all they can do is issue a ticket that will generate a fine. The weak legal powers of municipalities are reflected in the weak powers of municipal inspectors. Thus, if a city mayor or other authority decides to forcefully expel protesters and/or unhoused people from parks, they usually have to ensure that police are present and support the 'eviction' work of municipal inspectors. (This collaboration between police and municipal inspectors was seen in 2022 in the Toronto park of Trinity-Bellwoods, which had become a preferred spot for 'encampments', that is, groups of tents put up by unhoused people, much to the dismay of the then mayor, conservative John Tory).

Here I will limit the scope of the chapter to urban legal islands in Toronto, where I live and where I often conduct empirical research. And in so doing it makes sense to begin with what looks to outsiders as the most public space in the city, namely Yonge-Dundas square.[3]

After that we will go over some of the governance details of two other spaces that look eminently public but turn out to have unique governance structures – city hall square, also known as Nathan Phillips square, and the relatively new park space known as 'the Bentway'. The point of presenting these legally hybrid spaces as the main examples of 'city building' today is to reverse the usual municipal-law paradigm. Privately owned or privately managed public spaces are generally presented as exceptions, as unique and peculiar (often 'innovative') governance assemblages. But perhaps it is now finally time to show that the exception has become the rule, in that all manner of new initiatives now call on the 'urban legal island' set of tools. Park 'conservancies', for instance, designed with the model of New York's Central

3 Given the fact that Dundas street and Dundas square were named after British imperial official Henry Dundas, who played an ambiguous role in the British effort to abolish the maritime traffic in African enslaved peoples, there was in 2023 an effort to change the name of the square and that of the long street which it abuts. The committee charged with finding a new name chose an African name, Sankofa square, as the replacement. And yet, the name change did not get implemented. The incoming administration of progressive mayor Olivia Chow, who does not have to worry about her political capital in progressive circles the way that former Mayor John Tory (who initiated the name change) did, has not gone ahead with the re-naming.

Park in mind, remove a park that looks like a city park from the portfolio of the municipal parks department. And park conservancies are becoming increasingly popular, often under the banner of empowering neighbours to work with the city to govern their local parks.

The purpose of this chapter is thus to illustrate that although one can certainly isolate 'seeing like a city' as a distinct mode of governance, today the trend in urban redevelopment, and urban planning in general, centrally features hybrid entities that are officially recognized by city council and city hall staff but that are not ordinary public spaces such as municipal parks or ordinary sidewalks.

In that sense this chapter contributes to highlighting how, in urban planning and design, the supposed hard legal line separating public from private spaces has become so blurred as to have become somewhat meaningless. Many urban studies scholars have noted the powers either granted to or simply taken by private entities in urban development, and there is indeed a considerable literature on POPS (privately owned public spaces). Therefore the main argument of this chapter is not original, but it still poses radical challenges to law-school doctrines about 'public' vs 'private' powers, public vs private corporations and public vs private urban spaces.[4]

First Example of Urban Legal Island: Yonge-Dundas Square

> 'Can I propose to my partner on the Square? Can I have engagement photos taken?'
>
> [from the official website of Yonge-Dundas square in Toronto, ydsq.ca]

Answer [also on website]:

> If you are planning a simple down on one knee sort of proposal then of course! If you are looking for something dramatic, involving props or a cast of many people, then you would need to book the Square as if you were doing an event (which you are!), as it may impede our event executions. If it's just you, your partner and a ring then that's no problem. Personal photographs are allowed to be taken in the Square, but you have to work around the events and the general public, you can't section off an

4 One notable study that demonstrates the growing importance of private actors, developers and others, in the age we could call that of neoliberal urbanism, is Susan Feinstein, *The City Builders: Property Development in New York and London 1980–2000* (Blackwell 1994, second revised edition University Press of Kansas 2001).

> area or impede the activities of the Square. If you need props or lighting equipment (etc) then you will need to book the Square for a photo shoot (there are costs associated). For more information on photography and film shoots click here.

Clicking there takes you to the next section of the rules and regs, which specify rules about photography. Other than tourists using their personal cell phones to capture an informal moment with just a few people, which remains free and unregulated, photography requires a permit. That of course would apply to fancy, commercially mediated engagement or proposal events that were mentioned at the outset.

The website adds that drones and airplanes and anything aerial is prohibited. The official website mentions helipads in nearby hospitals, which would appear to justify banning drones – but that might be merely an excuse for more private control of the central urban space.

The Yonge-Dundas intersection is best known for the fact that it is the intersection with the highest pedestrian count in Canada, not just in Toronto. It is the location of the large indoor shopping centre known as the Eaton Centre. The naming persists even though the Eaton department store, which used to be the anchor shop in the mall and in many other shopping centres around Canada, has long departed not just the location but the Canadian marketplace.

As is implied in the requirement for permits to do things that are not offenses under any law, such as organizing informal 'sets' to act as background for wedding proposals, the square looks like a public space but is not legally public. The Yonge-Dundas square authority is publicly endorsed, but it is actually a semi-private body. Private security guards police the square, and rumour has it[5] that some of the mall's surveillance CCTV cameras are not pointed to the inside of the mall to record possible breaches of public order but are pointed outwards, so as to capture the images of the large numbers of pedestrians who are either going in or out of the mall or walking towards or away from nearby businesses, such as the large 'Best Buy' electronics store.

What is now the largely privatized square that looks as if it's a public gathering place is the result of a long process by which the city of Toronto began the 'regeneration' project by expropriating a row of marginal businesses along Yonge street just north of Dundas. The expropriation was contested, since at the time it was not strictly speaking legal for public bodies with expropriation

5 Undergraduate students working with me in years past, one of whom was the daughter of the gentleman with the security-camera contract for the mall, told me about the orientation of the security cameras, which capture pedestrians along Dundas street and Bay street, not just Yonge Street. No information is available publicly about the CCTV cameras. Hence my using the phrase 'rumour has it', even though the claims made in my undergraduate class in legal geography seem very well founded.

powers to take over privately owned real estate in order to sell it to other, preferred private owners.[6]

The sale went ahead, as Evelyn Ruppert's detailed study of the planning hearing explains.[7] But for a long time there was nothing but a big hole in the ground where the marginal businesses had stood, since the movie-theatre company that had bought the property (a property encompassing the locations of many small businesses) did not believe that the local consumer market would support yet another set of small theatres.

The 'hole in the ground' became a meaningful symbol in local politics – a symbol of municipal incompetence for some, of corporate malfeasance for others. I used to rike my bicycle to the university along Dundas Street, and I saw that the city had clearly authorized the private owner to interfere with the sidewalk and the streetcar stops. But I only knew that the property was privately owned due to research done by a York University graduate student who was working on a doctorate in sociology but had previously worked as an urban planner, Evelyn Ruppert.

Eventually the US-owned AMC company decided to go ahead and build the set of theatres. The US film theatre company pursued a 'partnership' with a local university whereby the university (then called Ryerson, now renamed TMU) would utilize the theatres in the morning, with films being shown in the afternoons and evenings.[8]

Second Example of Urban Legal Island: Nathan Phillips Square

The large concrete-covered space in front of the 'new' city hall (scare quotes used because 'new' is not so new, referring to the 1950s modernist behemoth that replaced 'Old city hall', a late nineteenth-century building nearby) is public, in the sense of publicly owned and publicly controlled and policed. It is considered by the citizens of the city as the eminent public space of the city. It hosts the annual New Year's Eve celebrations and many more or less

6 In the United States the Supreme Court ruled that municipalities could indeed expropriate 'non-blighted' property to sell to better private owners, in the *Kelo* decision out of New Jersey. But in the wake of this decision many states passed new statutes banning such an action, under the rationale of protecting the private owner rights of ordinary Americans. The issue remains contested.

7 Evelyn Ruppert, *The Moral Economy of Cities: Making Good Citizens* (Toronto, University of Toronto Press, 2006).

8 There is no publicly available information on the 'deal', such as the contract between AMC theatres and the university. Information used here is largely a result of personal communications and observation over several years. But see the complicated rules and regulations governing Dundas Square/Sankofa square, at https://www.ydsq.ca for a good example of the micro-management of apparently public spaces by 'public-private' partnerships.

spontaneous gatherings have taken place there, often after messages go out on social media and messaging platforms inviting people to participate in a protest or celebration.

Nevertheless that space has its own unique by-law.[9] Hence the space is legally unique. The rather fantastical fears of disorder of the legislators that created the by-law are all too clear in the particulars of the by-law. One provision states that ice skates can only be worn on the skating rink (a major tourist photo op) – as if anyone really desired to go on ice skates on the concrete of the square. Another states that public singing and speeches are prohibited, but there is an exception for poetry.

In addition, around 2009-10 the Nathan Phillips square by-law (Municipal Code 237) was amended to prohibit sleeping on the square – in a feeble effort to regulate the homeless citizens who had taken to sleeping in a sheltered area of the square. The unhoused citizens, perhaps influenced by the local discourse of diversity and inclusion, had begun to sleep under the concrete walkways around the square. The amendment to the by-law, however, was not enforced with any zeal (or maybe it was not enforced at all, local prominent civil rights lawyers not being able to name a single case).

The website of the square is similar to that for Yonge-Dundas. It explains that organizations seeking to use the square for events need to apply for a permit. Organizations and groups are not guaranteed that the permit will be granted. As is the case with other permits, it is not made publicdly clear what the criteria are. As of this writing, the square's listed official events include a 'Pillow Fight' (whose character remains mysterious) and a Canadian-Latin music fest, at the end of May 2025.

City officials, however, clearly exercise more control over Nathan Phillips square than over Yonge-Dundas square, with many of the events that are granted permits having some connection to the formal city hall power structure. Perhaps due to its connections, physical and symbolic, to city hall, the traditional use of the square for public protests is not totally sidelined in favour of commercial events, as has happened with Yonge-Dundas square.

For example: In late March 2025, a large public rally against Donald Trump's tariffs on Canadian products was held there – labelled an 'Elbows up' gathering – 'elbows up' being a hockey term recently adopted, in early 2025, for popular use, to encourage Canadian nationalism and a rejection of the Trump agenda. That rally was attended by the mayor. One assumes that permission for the rally involved the mayor's office granting itself permission for the rally, which also featured major pop musicians.

If we stop thinking of the distinction between public and private spaces in binary terms, and think more in terms of a spectrum, it is clear that

9 See toronto.ca, municipal code by-law 237, https://www.toronto.ca/wp-content/uploads/2019/07/8eb5-MC237-NPS.pdf

Nathan Phillips square is more public and arguably more democratic than Yonge-Dundas square, which appears to grant permits mainly to commercial enterprises.

Third Example of Urban Legal Island: The Bentway

The Bentway looks like a city park, but is clearly a 'premium' space. It has features that go beyond the standard somewhat drab facilities that generally exist in Toronto's parks. The Bentway is a legally unusual entity, created underneath a much-criticized highway, on land that was previously part of the Fort York historic site (and presumably controlled by the federal government, though ownership information is very hard to come by).

But despite its appearance, The Bentway is legally a 'Conservancy', which as mentioned above is a park that may be run by city officials or governed by city rules but that attracts philanthropic funding in a non-redistributive manner. It was created around 2017 with a $25m donation from local urbanist Judy Matthews. It has some paid jobs, though not many, and features 'special' events such as public art displays and festivals.

The original model for parks designated as 'conservancies' is New York's Central Park conservancy, briefly discussed in the previous chapter. Readers may recall that the model of a conservancy is not new, and can be traced back in US history to such innovations as the Carnegie libraries, set up as public-private partnerships long before that was a term.

The Conservancy model was designed to draw in philanthropic donations and keep them in that spot. This replicates for parks the way in which many American urban regeneration projects were designed, as public-private partnerships, with the private sector (the business community, usually) holding much more power than would be the case if strict democracy were observed.[10]

As already intimated in the previous chapter, the conservancy model ensures that the philanthropists/rich people who live near that particular 'conservancy' are able to donate funds that do not go into the city's coffers and are 'at risk' of being spent in far-flung racialized areas, but rather stay within that small central area. Often the philanthropists in question also dominate the board that makes decisions for the semi-private park (as they did in the numerous parks boards and library boards that were set up across the United

10 For the history of Central Park see Roy Rosenzweig, *The Park and the People: A History of Central* Park (Ithaca NY, Cornell University Press, 1992). The Conservancy was created in the 1990s and has been regarded as an early experiment in municipal privatization. But for earlier experiments in public-private partnerships that sought to improve only a designated area of the city, not the whole city, see Jon Teaford's multi-volume history of municipal government in the United States. The UK, in part because of the rise of the Labour party, had relatively few public-private partnerships until the Thatcher era. For a comparison of UK and US urbanism in the time period before the welfare state, see Richard Dennis, *Cities in Modernity* (Cambridge, 2008).

States in what one might call the golden age of private enterprise, otherwise known as the era of the 'robber barons').

Often volunteer resources flow as if by gravity to these 'conservancies', even though they might be far more useful in far-flung parks or playgrounds that serve largely racialized communities. And the Bentway definitely draws volunteers. It has a structure that enables volunteer training and deployment, unlike regular city parks, which often turn their backs on potential volunteers from the area due in part to labour union rules constraints.

The city parks department is rarely set up to include volunteers, a loss not only for the parks but for the people (especially young people) who might benefit from a volunteer position. And of course there are plenty of stories, in Toronto as in other cities, about the failings of the 'city bureaucracy' including the parks department.

Nevertheless the conservancy model has the practical and long-term effect of creating 'premium' spaces in the city, adding spatial inequality to the existing structures of socio-economic inequality. The Bentway is clearly one such space.[11] The Bentway is now engaged in creating what their website calls 'Bentway islands', which are meant to continue the Bentway, presumably with its governing structure intact, under other portions of the ugly Gardiner expressway.

Ideally, philanthropic as well as public resources would be more evenly spread across the city, which would help to counteract social and spatial inequalities. It may seem churlish to criticize philanthropists. However, one can witness the spread to other parts of the world of the American philanthropic model, which begins from the premise that public expenditures are not well spent on the poor and marginalized and are better spent on the symphony or the art gallery.

The Bentway includes as a founding 'partner' and aesthetic model the tri-government agency Waterfront Toronto, which has created numerous 'tiny perfect' parks and which I and my colleague Alex Flynn have written about at length.[12] Waterfront Toronto, like the Bentway, pays attention to Indigenous cultures and racialized artists, in keeping with the local norm of 'iversity and inclusion, and the national discourse of 'reconciliation' with First Peoples. But none of these tiny perfect entities are contributing any land to the 'land back' or 'money back' reparation claims circulated by Indigenous activists.[13]

11 See the very attractive to highly cultured and/or educated eyes images found in the 2023–2024 annual report of the Bentway, at https://thebentway.ca/publication/2023-2024-annual-report/

12 Alex Flynn and Mariana Valverde, 'Where the Sidewalk Ends: the Governance of Waterfront Toronto's Deal with Sidewalk Labs', *Windsor Yearbook of Access to Justice* (2019). Alexandra Flynn & Mariana Valverde (2019): Planning on the Waterfront: Setting the Agenda for Toronto's 'smart city' Project, *Planning Theory & Practice*, doi:10.1080/14649357.2019.1676566.

13 See the 'Red Papers' entitled *Land Back* and *Money Back* and publicly posted on the website of Toronto's Yellowhead Institute, a local Indigenous-led research unit based at Toronto Metro-

Cities all around the world are following the international trend that seeks not to overhaul the city itself, or to counteract the growing socio-economic and spatial inequalities that mark our cities, but rather to create some small 'innovative' spaces, premium spaces that tend to be located not randomly across the city but in areas that are frequented by certain upper classes.

And in doing so, city officials are unwittingly (or wittingly) contributing to the hollowing out of the public sector and the empowering of private sector actors (philanthropists as well as business people). The $25 million Canadian that could potentially have transformed several public spaces in areas such as Scarborough or South Etobicoke have been donated specifically for the Bentway – a premium space similar to New York City's Highline, a magnet for relatively wealthy tourists as well as locals who frequent locations rich in cultural capital.

Conclusion

Today it makes sense, I argue, to eschew the generalities about formal city planning and its failures, aesthetic and socio-economic. Instead of reifying city governance and constructing a binary division (seeing like a state vs. seeing like a city), it might be more suitable to think of the city's map as an archipelago formed by the coexistence of a large number of more or less private 'islands', weakly connected by a sea of generic public space. The 'sea' within which the islands exist is the non-premium generic municipal space that, not only in Toronto, shows much evidence of wear and tear, and is regarded as the only place where unhoused or street people should be.

In a city such as Toronto, unhoused people are largely tolerated. Once in a while there are instances of extreme violence against them, just as the Toronto police are every so often guilty of extreme violence against people in mental health crises or young Black men. But 'diversity is our strength' is the city's motto, and that has a certain weight and reflects a certain locally powerful ethic. However, empirical research shows that the much-vaunted diversity is often differentiated into 'good' diversity (racial diversity amongst professionals, for example) and 'bad' diversity (marked by the presence of visible drug users, unhoused people, panhandlers and sex workers).[14]

This chapter has argued that instead of seeking to identify an essence for 'seeing like a city', in contrast with other scales used for seeing space and governing it, it might be better to use the archipelago metaphor. It might be better to leave aside the welfare-state ideal of an urban space where redistribution takes place and the poor as well as the rich have legal rights, since such

politan University (TMU).

14 See Mariana Valverde, 'The Ethic of Diversity: Local Law and the Negotiation of Urban Norms' *Law and Social Inquiry* vol. 33 no. 4 (Fall 2008), 895–924.

an ideal has long ceased to reflect how cities actually 'do' things, as the wide-ranging literature on neoliberal urbanism has shown. The emphasis on 'innovative partnerships' that one sees everywhere in urbanism today suggests that micro-local improvements are what is privileged today. Jane Jacobs taught generations of planners to value the neighbourhood. But Jacobs was writing in the 1950s and 1960s, at the height of welfare-state and democratic ideals. Today urbanists and city officials alike are far more likely to focus on micro-local projects. In this endeavour to generate some 'premium' spaces, leaving the rest of the city looking more drab and grey by comparison. Micro-local improvement projects, such as the tiny perfect parks that Waterfront Toronto has been building along the waterfront, often containing interesting public art, greatly increase the market value of the condos that are the main type of building on the waterfront.

Urbanism today is all about 'innovation and entrepreneurship' (a slogan favored today by the University of Toronto), and hence the micro-local scale of the special, premium space dominates. There are still numerous 'regular' public parks, and the Toronto Transit Commission does its best to provide public transit throughout the city. To put it differently, the 'neoliberal city', as many critical urbanists have dubbed it, is not a homogeneous space where policy is enacted throughout the territory of the legal city. It is an archipelago in which some 'nice' buildings and nice public spaces stand out as urban legal islands. The value granted to 'innovation' and to 'partnerships' has the effect of encouraging public-private partnerships, and that is often a method for concentrating public as well as private money in certain micro spaces, spaces that are by no means randomly chosen or based on evidence of need.

5 The Scale of the Family Household

Not everyone lives in a family household – and yet there is a somewhat ideological identification or confusion of 'family' with 'household'. The term 'ideological' is appropriate because the fact is that many families are spread out over several households (as in the case of divorced parents). And of course a household can easily be composed of people who are not related. These are not always university students living with roommates. In some cities, high rental prices have encouraged many singles who might prefer to live alone to try to find compatible roommates. If the roommate or roommates prove compatible, the single person who chooses to live with others may be able to live in a convenient location at a reasonable price.

In recent years, the identification of 'family' with 'household' (or rather the slippage, since those two terms are not synonymous, having different meanings) has become particularly out of touch with demographic realities. The key fact questioning the identification of household with family is that the proportion of single-person households has been rapidly increasing, especially in big cities, over the past decade or two. The 2020 Census of the United States recorded the highest share of single-person households ever, at over 27%. This is in striking contrast to 1940, when only 7.7% of households were single-person ones.

In the United States especially but also in other places, a large, often the largest part of the single-person households are those of elderly singles, especially widows, who on the average live longer than men. But that proportion of single-person households has not radically changed recently, whereas the proportion of people who are no longer of college age but remain unattached has grown significantly.

In Canada, the 2016 census recorded 29% of households as single-person units. There were nevertheless marked differences across the country, reflecting broader differences in both cultural preferences and notions of kinship. Quebec had the highest rate of single-person households, likely due to the prevalence of separated and divorced people there. (The proportion of 'never married' people is higher in Quebec than in other provinces).

DOI: 10.4324/9781003612551-6

By contrast, Nunavut, a mostly Inuit (formerly 'Eskimo') territory in the far North, had the lowest rate of single-person households in 2016. This is probably because of the severe housing shortage in the far North, but it also reflects the social acceptability in the far North, especially among Inuit and First Nations, of multigenerational and other non-nuclear family households.[1] In many First Nations communities aunts or grandmothers often take over the parenting of young children.

But regardless of numbers and statistics, which are obviously different from country to country, the family household is still a key experience for most people. More importantly, it is an experience – and an institution – that is deeply imbued with sentiment. Those sentiments help to shape urban planning practices, as well as contributing to stigmatizing those who do not fit the family-household ideal.

Most of us grow up in a family household. Even for those of us who do not, as is the case for the increasing numbers of children in high-divorce jurisdictions, the desires for safety and unconditional love associated in family households, as well as the expectation of unconditional financial support that characterize the family household (at least in theory) often haunt us well into old age.

One consequence of the long-term cultural preference, in most Western countries, for nuclear family households has been the decline of collective 'solutions', such as orphanages, which were numerous in the nineteenth century and into the early twentieth century. Foster parents are nowadays everywhere preferred to institutions, even though fostering is not always the best solution for the individual child or youth, particularly if foster parents are in it mainly for the money the state provides.

Western European countries, such as Germany, Norway and Finland have even higher rates of single-person households than the United States and Canada. Arguably the statistics may be marking an epochal demographic shift whereby millenials are not forming stable couples and/or are not having children until relatively late in life. Even in Spain, where it is considered normal for adult children who remain unmarried to live with their parents, the rate of single-person households approaches 26%.

Some research also points to the fact that young women often want to be established in their careers before going on maternity leave. That factor, combined with a lack of affordable housing in most large cities, results in couples often postponing having children until later than was the case for the previous generation.

1 Many First Nations children in Canada, and Aboriginal children in Australia, are reared and cared for by their grandmothers, not their biological parents. The reasons for this are complex and not within the scope of this book.

Elderly widows have often lived alone, historically. I might make sense to treat elderly widows as a separate category rather than including them in the vague category of 'single-person households'. What is new in demographic news is the proportion of adults, 35–44, who are living alone. That proportion, to use a current media cliché, is unprecedented. And yet, despite demographic and economic realities, the ideological bond that links 'family' (nuclear family in particular) to 'household' stays strong. There are many reasons for this continuing identification.

As feminist scholarship has long pointed out, the family household is often imagined to be a 'haven in a heartless world' (to use US sociologist Christopher Lasch's influential terminology). That is the golden glow that attaches to the institution. The *experiences* of families and households, on the other hand, are all too often not in keeping with the 'haven in a heartless world' ideology. Most gender violence takes place within the home, as research studies across a wide variety of jurisdictions has shown. And often, the culprits are precisely those older males that generations of girls, across most countries and cultures, have been taught to regard as their 'natural' protectors. Predatory males, research studies show, are usually not the 'strangers' featured in American murder mysteries and TV police procedurals but rather girls' older brothers, stepbrothers, stepfathers and fathers, as well as uncles and grandfathers.

For many girls and women, therefore, the family household is anything but a place of safety. It is no 'haven in a heartless world', except for some lucky women and children. The family household is all too often a dangerous place, perhaps the most dangerous place.

What can be said from the perspective of legal geography about the family household? The late great British feminist geographer Doreen Massey was one of many who helped to move the study of the scale of the family household beyond the 1950s cliches about the home as the place characterized by love and safety – what one might call, if one focuses on the physical arrangements, the white picket-fence ideal.

One feature of the actual household that runs contrary to the mythical image of the 'haven' is the way in which different temporal scales mark the lives of different household members, often divided by gender (and generation, though this is less studied, the mobility challenges of teens living in suburbs not being a major area of scholarly interest). One early British study that shows what legal geography can do if gender is taken into account was of a town where the men were largely employed as scientists in a nearby major university. The men consistently enjoyed a largely global scale of intellectual exchange, at the office and even at home (when on e-mail or on phone calls with far-flung colleagues). The wives, in sharp contrast in terms of scale, were almost all housewives.

Most of the wives lived in a far narrower world, a world punctuated by school runs, school weekly schedules and seasonal shifts, and such mundane activities that are highly local in scale, such as grocery shopping trips. The spatial scales of the household thus depended more or less completely on which gender one belonged to. (Nowadays many women have professional jobs, but the study was conducted at a time when scientific work was nearly all male and almost all faculty wives were housewives). Globalization and instant communications shaped the men's lives, therefore, while women remained confined to a far more local scale.

Massey was very attentive to spatial scales: but like other professional geographers she often neglected the temporal scales that are as important in daily experience as the spatial scales.[2] Temporally, nuclear-family households can be said to have several overlapping scales. First there is the daily scale of going to work (for the employed adults) and going to school (for the children), with both generations returning home (typically for dinner, in Anglo cultures). Then there is the weekly scale of weekdays vs. weekends, with markedly different expectations about how time is spent and what spaces are used. Finally there is the seasonal scale of summer children's sports, summer barbecues with family friends and relatives, family summer holidays (often taken by means of the 'family' car) and so on.

The interesting contrast here is that the activities typical of summer for each nuclear family household are distinct from those typical of the winter, which means that sociological studies that do not account for the seasons can be deficient. Depending on the place, winter might involve ice skating, skiing, ice hockey, tobogganing or indoor sports like basketball. The 1950s and 1960s housewife had to be very attentive to the changing seasons, whereas the husband, the 'man in a grey flannel suit', could largely ignore the seasons, since his workplace did not significantly change with the seasons. But the breadwinner husband/father also shared in the nuclear family's leisure activities, and to that extent he too experienced seasonal and weekly cycles.

A particular example of how time is not homogeneous is Christmas. A special place is generally made on the yearly household calendar for Christmas, which since Dickens' time has been the family household holiday par excellence. Even Jewish and Hindu households often 'get into' what is generally called 'the spirit of Christmas, or 'the spirit of the season', in a rather vain effort to acknowledge the existence of non-Christians.

My Jewish Austrian grandfather, a good example of assimilation into the Christian culture of Austria at the time (around 1900–1910), loved nothing

2 Numerous sources across a wide range of disciplines explore the spatializations and temporalizations of law. One useful source is Philip Steinberg, 'Blue Planet, Black Lives: Matter, Memory and the Temporalities of Political Geography' *Political Geography* vol. 96 (2022) at 10524. For more theoretical work in this line, see Alexandre Lefebvre, *The image of Law: Deleuze, Bergson Spinoza* (Stanford University Press, 2008) and Elizabeth Grosz, *Space, Time and Perversion: Essays on the Politics of Bodies* (London, Routledge 2018).

better than a 'Tannenbaum', that is an evergreen Christmas tree, complete with real candles. His family household including his ten children sang German Christmas carols with great abandon, even after they found out, relatively late in life, that he was Jewish).

Spatial scales and temporal scales, whether of family life or of household routines, or both, are not completely separate. In other words: time and space are not distinct variables in sociologists' sense of the word. How exactly they are intertwined depends on the situation.

Christmas in an Anglo, Protestant, white, middle-class household is perhaps a great example of almost completeoverlap. Spatial habits (sitting down for Christmas dinner, for example, often in the same spot as in other years) coincide very neatly with holiday temporalities: the Christmas dinner is often taken at a time that is the same from year to year, unlike regular weekday dinners whose timing often varies according to the various activities of household members. On Christmas day, there are no hobbies or sports or friends' gatherings that compete with nuclear-family life. The nuclear family 'chronotope' can be supreme, for that one day.

To reinforce the coterminous nature of special-holiday temporal and spatial scales, the cast of characters at the dinner is usually also the same. To compound the homogeneity or sameness of the yearly celebration, the family stays indoors for almost the whole day (with a short family walk sometimes ritually included, or, in snowy climates, an outing for the kids to burn off calories). Christmas day life is remarkably similar across neighbourhoods, varying only by ethnic and religious identities.

Some families/households may have a certain TV or radio program that marks 'Christmas', such as her late majesty Elizabeth II's annual Christmas message, which was devoutly listened on the radio for decades in households throughout the Commonwealth. The interruption of the almost sacred time-space of the family household – especially during Christmas day, which since Dickens' time has been celebrated as a great domestic holiday, not so much a specifically Christian one – by the Queen's message could be regarded as the eruption of a transnational scale into the much more limited scale of the family household. But the Queen herself never failed to mention her own husband and children in that annual speech, a mention that would have been 'out of place' in state-related events such as the speech from the throne at the opening of each Parliament.[3] (The peculiar spatial and temporal scales

3 Whether the current King Charles's Christmas message is listened to with the same reverence on as that garnered by his late mother is not yet known as of this writing. Nevertheless, anecdotally, 'The Commonwealth' seems less interested in royal family rituals under King Charles than it was under the late Queen.

of royal life have not been empirically studied as far as I know, for obvious reasons of access.)[4]

At other times, especially if the wife has a demanding job, the temporal scales and the spatial scales of the household may not quite coincide. If the wife has to pick up kids from a carer, and/or run home to get dinner ready, she may be in a real hurry and feel anxious and stressed as a result, which may negatively affect her mothering. It is probable that she will constantly feel as if there isn't time for ordinary life – and this is no mere feeling. Plenty of empirical studies have shown that wives continue to do most of the housework even if they have full-time jobs. Fathers, on the other hand, typically take a more relaxed view of both childrearing and housework. I am not the only feminist professor who has male colleagues who pride themselves on being 'involved' fathers but who rarely cook (other than managing the barbecue – barbecuing being the only form of cooking gendered masculine, which in Canada has the effect of confining masculine cooking to the short summer months).

But despite the anxieties and stresses and tempooral conflicts of parenting and housework that dominate many family households (especially those with small children), the family household continues to enjoy a romantic, nostalgic rosy glow. One symptom of the persistent romantic glow of 'the family household' is that adults often ask one another if they are going 'home' for the holidays – as if their family of origin forever stood at the forefront of emotional significance, regardless of actual experiences. Queer and trans people are particularly disadvantaged in this regard. They may have a 'chosen family' made up mostly of other queer and/or trans folks, but annual holiday plans rarely feature such 'chosen' families.

Race and ethnicity also play a major role in organizing the family household. Mixed marriages (as they are still called) are increasingly common; but the family household has to somehow decide which holidays to celebrate and which to ignore. Further, inviting relatives – as many households with children do for holiday family dinners and/or summer barbecues – becomes somewhat fraught when race or ethnic differences present 'the family' with different sets of relatives brought up with different holiday or everyday rituals. How actually existing families cope with these demands, which pull them in different directions, is being studied now by anthropologists and sociologists of 'the family', but we do not yet have enough data for generalizations.

One can therefore say that the ideology of the nuclear family seldom recognizes race or sexual orientation as factors that can divide the family household, or potentially divide them, even though biographies and autobiographies and realistic novels that document these contradictory pulls and resulting disputes are numerous.

4 That 'the Crown' enjoys the peculiar ability to be in many places at the same time is one of its features.

Given the many differences between the mythical breadwinner nuclear family and actual families, it may be useful to follow in the footsteps of US late lesbian feminist poet Adrienne Rich, who famously wrote a book on how the institution of motherhood differs from the actual experience of having children.[5] Adapting Rich's terminology, it is useful to distinguish the ideology or institution of 'the family' from the many experiences that people have.

Adrienne Rich's influential 1976 book *Of Woman Born* begins with a harrowing story about a white American woman who killed her own children. One would not normally expect a book with 'motherhood' as its topic begin with such an 'unnatural' crime, but that is precisely the point. Delving with much insight into the negative feelings that most mothers at one point or another have about their children, Rich highlights that the institution of motherhood is ritually infused with a warm glow, but that the experiences of motherhood are many and often contradictory. That point has been made since her book was published about gender, about race and racism, and about a whole variety of other sacred cultural cows – 'the family' included.

But what legal geography can add to studies from cultural studies, philosophy, anthropology and other fields is to stress the close relationship, indeed the identification that is often unconsciously made between the two terms of 'family and 'household'. Household is a technical-sounding census term: but 'the family' continues, despite decades of feminist thought, to be suffused with a warm glow, even among people who have not had pleasant childhoods.[6]

The fact that a certain shape and type of building is considered, even by condo-dwelling inner-city kids, to be the archetypal family house (two windows, a peaked red roof, a front door in the middle) is not an accident. Children's drawings in a highly diverse city turn out to be remarkably similar if they are asked to picture 'a home'. 'Single-family detached' is everywhere in North America the A1 category of zoning law –the category subject to the least spatial restrictions.[7] That classification is rooted in the warm-glow ideology of the nuclear family household.

5 Adrienne Rich, *Of Woman Born: Motherhood as Experience and as Institution* (New York City, WW Norton, 1976).

6 Countless novels by women writers, English and non-English, from Jane Austen to Zadie Smith, document the lives of girls and women, especially the aspects of those experiences that are not reflected in formal planning or land-use law. For an influential overview of feminist legal geography see Doreen Massey, *Space, Place and Gender* (Polity Press and University of Minnesota Press, 1994).

7 See Constance Perin, *Everything in its Place: Social Order and Land Use in America* (Princeton University Press, 1977). Despite its age – and the fact that Oliver Sacks, an author far more famous than Perin, published a book with the same title – this is still one of the best ethnographic accounts of the social and moral values embedded in American land use regulation. It documents in painstaking detail the ideology that identifies a proper home with a single-family detached house filled with no people except those in a nuclear family.

Legal geography is concerned with governance *through* space as well as the governance *of* space. Both are at hard at work in the 'single-family detached' planning category that is even today the most 'sacred cow' of urban planning. The single-family detached home is furthermore supposed to contain only a nuclear family and always a nuclear family. Grandparents may be present, but if so the land use may require a formal exception – as has happened in the Greater Toronto area to many South Asian and East Asian multi-generational families, who are in the position of having to ask official permission to build the kind of house that would accommodate their particular family.[8]

The classic nuclear family is the social-moral-financial unit that is meant to be held completely in the container that land-use law calls 'single-family detached'. Other forms of housing obviously exist, and millions of families are adequately housed in apartments in many cities (Paris, Barcelona, Madrid, Rome). But in the ideology or the institution of the nuclear family, whose typical or characteristic temporal and spatial scales have been described above, the suburban ideal still prevails.

A recent study based on interviews with actually existing families in Vancouver shows how the suburban ideal persists even where and when it is totally unrealistic (due to the extreme prices for detached housing in the Vancouver area, not to mention the smaller households that are prevalent today).[9] As Adrienne Rich said about motherhood, the institution (of the nuclear family, and of the single-family detached form) lives on, even if real experiences are highly fragmented and contradictory.

In legal geography special attention is paid to local-level regulation, whether it be street vending by-laws, sidewalk-regulation by-laws and ordinances, or planning rules. That is because of the privileged place that urban space has in both geography as a discipline (where 'local' is often conflated with 'urban', to the detriment of rural life) and in modern Western experience. Privileging living in the most dense cities is not a merely Western preference, however. China's system of classifying cities into tiers, with increasing privileges going to Tier One cities and then Tier Two cities, could be used as an example of state-level legal geography, since the classification is made by the party-state, not the locality.

8 A similar situation that points to the 'normalization' of city spaces and city streets and buildings through urban planning rules that seem person-neutral takes place when mosques have to ask special official permission to have their building facing Mecca, or build a tall tower from where an imam can call the faithful to prayer. The fact that special permissions are required for mosques but not for Christian churches and Christian households underpins the normalizing character of city-law rules.

9 Inter alia, see Nathan Lauster, *The Death and Life of the Single-Family Home: Lessons From Vancouver for a More Livable City* (Philadelphia, Temple University Press, 2016).

Hence the relevance to legal geography of ethnographic studies of families and households such as Lauster's and Perin's, cited above. Empirical studies of such phenomena as the confinement of congregate living (including even retirement homes) to arterial roads, so that they do not impinge on the 'residential' character of streets. The term 'residential' is more limited than one might think. Streets zoned 'residential' are or are meant to be mainly full of single-family homes. What is remarkable about such rules relegating congregate living or non-family living to the major roads is that they seem to be class-neutral. Rooming houses and shelters may be affected by them, but so are upscale retirement homes, at least in the city where I live.

This goes back to the 1920s (in North America), when the American writer Clarence Perrin invented the 'neighbourhood unit'. The neighbourhood unit was and still is an entity that had already been privileged in the English 'garden suburb' notion, although the nomenclature remained distinct.

A neighbourhood unit as theorized by Perry was to be composed of a couple of thousand families living in single-family-detached ticky-tacky boxes.[10] Household life was meant to be focused on the elementary school at the centre of each neighbourhood unit. Even churches were confined to the edges, along with shopping venues.

The neighbourhood unit, at least the ideal one drawn by Perry, featured internal walkways, so that children could walk to school on their own without encountering traffic. There was literally no place in the neighbourhood unit for apartments or for such 'land uses' as homes collectively housing teens in state care or disabled people.

The neighbourhood unit persisted in law and in official plans even in the face of the massive apartment building construction of the post-World War II period. Indeed, it still exists in Toronto's local law, where 'apartment neighbourhoods' are rigidly separated from real neighbourhoods.

The real estate industry, likely more than law, is a major promoter of myths about both family and household life. For real estate agents, living in an apartment is meant to be confined to the extremes of the age pyramid. Young people just starting out and elderly couples and singles are the only 'demographics' to whom apartments and condos are marketed. The current North American real estate term 'empty nesters' is a wonderful example of the tyranny of the ideology of the nuclear family as well as the tyranny of the single-family detached house. In Toronto, condos for sale are marketed either to young professionals and/or to 'empty nesters' – as if once the kids are grown up and leave 'home', parents are left without meaning in life, just staring at an empty nest. (The metaphor of the family of origin as a 'nest' could

10 There are numerous studies, sociological and historical, of middle-class suburbs. One recently re-issued early critique of suburban planning and suburban ideology is Ian Nairn's 1955 *Outrage* (reprinted in London, 2024, by Notting Hill Press).

use some cultural studies critical analysis, but we will leave that for another day.) The grown-up children, in turn, may have jobs or may be doing a PhD, and yet even though they have not lived with their parents for a significant time, even years, they often face questions such as 'are you going home for Christmas'? That question presupposes that wherever they live currently is not 'home'.

In the interests of what is now often called 'experiential' learning, I would here recommend that students reading this book stop for a moment and take a close look at the official plans for the municipality they or their parents live in. Law students in particular are very unlikely to have studied by-laws and ordinances, but poring over by-laws may prove more educational than any second-hand accounts of other people's research.

Asking critical questions about the social and moral and political values embedded in the official plan and its categories is likely the best way to discover for oneself some curious facts about the legal geography of time and of place. And as for law students, if they go on to read a few of the empirical studies of local law and local law enforcement that exist, that will certainly help to fill what is very likely a big gap in their education. 'Big' law – constitutional law, international law – is not representative of law in general – as chapters 2, 3, 4 and 5 demonstrate.

Conclusion

This chapter has not proceeded in the format familiar from countless law review articles, with clearly marked sections following an initial summary of 'the literature' and an identification of the 'gap' in existing literature that the article seeks to fill.[11]

Instead, this chapter, even more than the previous ones, has wandered or meandered over some of the numerous issues that legal geography can help to illuminate, at the scale of the 'family-household'. The method followed to write this chapter has therefore emulated that identified by French philosopher Michel Certeau, who distinguished taking walks through cities from the bird's eye view favoured by mapmakers.It was Michel de Certeau who pointed out that walking around a city provides a very different kind of knowledge than the bird's eye view that either literally or metaphorically is preferred by most

11 For a critique of the format generally used in scholarly articles (not only those in law reviews), see Mariana Valverde, 'How the Academy Negatively Affects Writing Practice' *Northern Ireland Legal Quarterly* vol. 76 no. 2 (2025), no page numbers available, and Mariana Valverde, 'Between a Rock and a Hard Place: Beyond Both Disciplinarity and Interdisciplinarity', *Critical Analyses of Law*, vol. 1 no. 1 (2014), available at ISSN 2291-9732. The latter article argues for a return to pre-discipline, pre-nineteenth-century knowledge formats, somewhat ironically dubbed 'infra-disciplinarity'.

academics. The bird's-eye view embedded in maps – and in 'high theory', the kind of theory that assumes a scale of 30,000 feet altitude – seems 'objective', and comprehensive, but it simply lets us see some objects while neglecting or invisibilizing others. What de Certeau called the bird's-eye-view is not much different from what the feminist cultural critic Donna Haraway has called the 'god's eye view'. That legal scholarship might seek to be 'objective' and comprehensive may mean nothing but a choice of the kind of scale that is either a bird's-eye-view or a god's-eye-view.

Perhaps the most important point that readers should take away from this chapter is encouragement to help each reader question the supposedly natural or transhistorical bond that more or less firmly (depending on the jurisdiction) ties a particular form of social life (the nuclear patriarchal family, in this chapter's case) to a particular built form (the single-family detached house). The scale of the family household is meant to coincide with the scale of a particular kind of building (a building of a certain size and internal order plus 'premises' such as lawns and garages). Until the late 1960s or thereabouts, commercial moving companies often arbitrarily assigned a household's belongings to different boxes: some were labelled 'kitchen' or 'living room', which is sensible, but children's belongings were rigidly organized into 'boy's bedroom' and 'girl's bedroom'. Similarly, the 'family car' beloved of suburban households in the postwar period continued to send subliminal messages about the number and gender of the children parents were meant to have. Somewhat later parents began to feel that they needed to buy a minivan if they had more than one child, or even just one. That again is an unexplored kind of legal geography. We need more empirical and theoretical studies of the family car and of the 1980s and 1990s minivan that became almost mandatory in middle-class white North America.

Laws, often local but sometimes at higher levels (states or regions or provinces), tend to enshrine in law itself a particular hierarchy of households. This is done in part by relying on the culturally specific assumptions of both the nuclear patriarchal family and the single-family-detached category of land use, the bond between the two being readily visible in the typical child's drawing of 'a house'.[12] Because laws regulating land uses are usually local and are regarded, especially in law schools, as 'minor' or not important, law students are rarely exposed to critical accounts of both law and the culturally specific hierarchies that pervade both British and North American legal rules

12 It is remarkable that despite the contemporary proliferation of different types of both housing and family forms, children tend to draw 'a house' as if everyone lived in single-family detached homes. I observed this in my children's daycare, when they were small: the daycare included a large diversity of family forms, and likely also housing forms, but their drawings were remarkably similar. I do not exempt myself from this observation: my own two children grew up in a two-mom household, but when they played 'house' they reproduced heterosexual forms of parenting and home ownership.

for what planning law calls 'land uses'. The antipodes of British origin tend to follow in the footsteps of English law, and so this chapter applies to New Zealand and Australia too – with some differences, but many similarities as well.

A key element in contemporary land-use law is that, in theory, land-use law is not meant to regulate people – it is only meant to regulate land uses. Planning textbooks are full of injunctions about zoning and other local rules not being meant to regulate categories of person, as vagrancy laws did for centuries.

The mantra 'land use planning is about land uses, not persons' continues to ring throughout planning programs and textbooks. But even a slight acquaintance with legal geography's insights suggests that regulating land uses indirectly governs categories of people differentially. Those not living in a nuclear family, especially, often live in places (from expensive condos to homeless shelters) that are strictly regulated as to their location. The particulars differ from one jurisdiction to another, but everywhere 'residential' is the A1 category of zoning, the one with the least restrictions.

Law is therefore highly implicated in urban phenomena that might appear as the result of the 'free market' in real estate, such as the congregation of tall condo buildings on particular streets and particular portions of those streets.

Legal geography, especially when combined with critical studies of race and gender as key factors in local law, can offer tools and insights that could perhaps lead to law schools and law textbooks being more open to critical studies of 'space and place', and of the role that governing spaces and places (and temporalities) plays in the reproduction of socioeconomic inequalities.

Rules governing the height, mass and the legal uses of particular buildings are generally local. The concept of 'land use' enables a regulation of private choices that would not be tolerated in, say, corporate law contexts. If a mechanic's shop is defined as a commercial land use it will be admitted into a residential area only as a 'legal nonconforming' use – an interesting category that has no parallels in most other areas of law. Cities in the Anglosphere developed zoning and other rules at a time (1930s–1950s, mainly) that enshrined in law hierarchical classifications of both humans and human activity that reflected the values of those with power – the hegemonic values as some neo-Marxists say.

One of the many consequences of the widespread adoption of zoning and similar rules about 'land uses' is that minority practices (having a multi-generational family in a single dwelling, for example, or running a business out of one's home) can be tolerated but only as exceptions. Mosques in Toronto and other English-speaking cities did not fall afoul of general rules banning minarets (as was the case in Switzerland). But if they wanted to comply with religious rules and associated cultural practices, they had to appear before a board of zoning appeals that might possibly allow them to depart from the law in the books, say by having a mosque face Mecca rather than being perpendicular to the street. The board of zoning appeals or its equivalent is what Foucault would have called a technique of normalization. Exceptions can be and often are made; but that just tells us in no uncertain terms who can exercise their culturally specific choices 'as of right', and who instead is subject to an often stigmatizing process of exceptionalization.

Casting a broader look beyond common-law jurisdictions, we can say that local law is culturally biased – even more strongly than state law (such as criminal law, or constitutional law). The governance of city spaces, both public and private, and the governance of people and activities through space, are rarely challenged as discriminatory in constitutional law. This is partly because local jurisdictions tend to cut and paste from other localities instead of starting from scratch, so that a judge would be loath to strike down a rule that seems local but exists throughout the country or even the continent. But it is also because local rules, especially planning rules, rarely have a rational justification. They simply are – 'we've always done it this way'. The non-rational character of local law was brought to me very clearly when about fifteen years ago I was interviewing city lawyers involved in planning, and I asked for the reason behind a seemingly arbitrary rule, such as a 330 meter separation distance between two establishments that were instances of a 'problem' non-preferred business. The city official told me, 'oh, when Canada went metric we had to change the 1,000 feet separation distances to metric, and that gave us what look like weird numbers'.

Pragmatism and the search for compromises among neighbours in conflict, rather than the implementation of a rational, logical plan are what make local law local. But all along, the values inherent in the rules remain unchallenged. There are of course exceptions, such as one sees in official plans that would instal alleyways in suburban tract housing rather than driveways. The quest to restore some mythical image of 'downtown' life – what could be more urban than an alleyway? – can gather a lot of support, at least among minority groups. But exceptions are so essential to the workings of a system that ultimately perpetuates the middle-class ideal of a suburban, patriarchal nuclear family that one has to conclude that the ease with which exceptions are or at least can be granted only ensures that the rules themselves are seldom challenged.

6 The Scale of the Human Body

Other than in work by queer legal geographers, which is limited in scope and numerical strength, one is unlikely to come across work that addresses powers and knowledges, especially assemblages in legal networks, from the point of view of the human body. Work by Black feminist scholars, some specifically analyzing power exercised through spatial means, is starting to undermine that generalization, but in turn the new Black geography tends to ignore queer work on space and power.[1]

Nevertheless, the human body and especially the bodies of women and trans people have become a major site of legal struggles in recent years. It is useful to focus on two examples of controversial issues concerning women's right to choose on abortion as well as the recent attacks on trans rights, especially trans youth rights, since they illustrate important general insights about bodily conduct and socio-cultural fears.

Issues pertaining to bodies and the legal status of humans who have certain bodies have become major dividing points in what many Americans call a 'culture war' – but without much factual knowledge about these bodies and their human subjects being made readily available. In other words, in the 'post-fact' or post-truth era, certain kinds of bodies have generated major moral panics, even if their numbers – especially the low numbers of trans people in the 'general' population, but even the number of women who might at any one point be seeking abortions – would not seem to justify any major policy or legal response.

It is therefore appropriate to begin this chapter by recounting the story of how the US Supreme Court moved recently (June 2022) to throw out the

1 There is relevant work – not necessarily put forward as legal geography but of relevance – based on Black women's embodiment (both objectively and subjectively). For two recent review essays of the relatively new field of Black women's geography see Alex Moulton and Inge Salo, 'Black Geographies and Black Ecologies as Insurgent Ecocriticism' *Environment and Society* vol. 13 no. 1 (2022), 156–174, and Camilla Hawthorne, 'Black Matters are Spatial Matters: Black Geographies for the Twenty-First Century' *Geography Compass* vol. 13 no. 11 (Nov. 2019). Both credit Katherine McKrittick's foundational work *Demonic Grounds* (Minneapolis, University of Minnesota Press, 2006).

DOI: 10.4324/9781003612551-7

'privacy' law doctrine that has for a long time been seen by US courts as central to constitutional litigation and that had, among other things, legally protected women's right to choose whether to abort or to carry a pregnancy to term.

Roe v Wade, decided in 1973 at the Supreme Court of the United States, was the landmark case widely taken (by feminists as well as by their enemies) as guaranteeing women's legal right to choose on abortion. This was despite the fact that notwithstanding the many legal and especially constitutional rights available to citizens of and in the United States, declarations of legality or illegality were not necessarily accompanied by moves to make practical access to abortion care (and pregnancy care) a reality across the land.[2] Some feminists were unhappy that a woman's right to choose was tethered so tightly to a distinctly liberal and individualistic notion of 'privacy', however. Socialist feminist thinkers, such as Rosalind Petchesky and Linda Gordon, reminded other American feminists that the American-law notion of 'privacy' was firmly rooted, philosophically and legally, in John Locke's idea that humans own their own bodies. Petchesky and Gordon highlighted Locke's notorious individualism. But more recent contributions, especially by Indigenous and postcolonial feminists, stress the distinctly settler-colonial and capitalist overtones of Locke's notion of legal personhood. The notion of self-ownership was a crucial legal and philosophical building block of wage-labour and hence of capitalism, it was pointed out. Tying a woman's right to choose to capitalist notions of privacy and self-ownership[3] was regarded as philosophically problematic, therefore. And yet there was wide agreement amongst feminists that the concept of 'privacy' was pragmatically useful, given the prevalence and legal power of liberal ideals in the United States. Pragmatism won the day, not only in *Roe v Wade* but in the 'successor' case, *Planned Parenthood v Casey* (1992). Neither of those two crucial decisions made overtly feminist moves, and both of them empowered women's doctors, who were largely male, as well as empowering women. It was the empowerment of women to make their own decisions that was highlighted by both proponents of *Roe v Wade* and *Planned Parenthood* and their latter-day critics. (The Vatican, on its part, continued to put forward a conservative notion

2 For a thorough discussion not only of Roe v Wade but of US abortion politics and theories of liberal law in the days when that decision prevailed, see Rosalind Petchesky, *Abortion and Women's Choice: The State, Sexuality and Reproductive Freedom* (Boston, Northeastern University Press, 1973).

3 The constitutional right to privacy is not in the actual Constitution of the United States. It emerged in the context of the professionalization of medical practice, especially around childbirth, where physicians attending birthing women in their homes had legal boundaries on their movements within the household and the resulting sightlines placed upon them. In early cases, however, the husband was not usually present, so it is difficult to know if 'privacy' was regarded as a right of the marital couple (as was the case when contraception was legalized) or a right of the woman herself.

of marriage and the nuclear family, and rejected women's autonomy in large part because that autonomy was generally seen as empowering individual women.) The Vatican held on to the myth of the nuclear family discussed in the previous chapter, and opposed contraception, not just abortion, under the banner of upholding 'natural' processes of reproduction, not to mention conservative notions of sexuality whereby potential reproduction was the only valid justification for heterosexual sex.

Nevertheless, since *Roe v Wade* essentially legalized abortion and made it very difficult for state legislatures (often wielding the powerful, in the United States, claim of 'state's rights') to claw back portions of this legal right, feminists and most Americans, according to opinion polls, accepted its terms. Speaking on a liberal podcast on American public radio (*Democracy Now*), well before the 2022 decision that reversed both *Roe* and *Planned Parenthood*, the former head of the US Coalition for Abortion Rights (CARAL) mused to Amy Goodman, the host of the show, that perhaps too much effort had gone into high-level constitutional litigation. She acknowledged that poor women and women of colour might have preferred a strategy that put practical access and funding ahead of constitutional litigation. That did not happen, in large part because of the powerful vested interests that in the United States have long fought against universal health insurance and continue to do so despite the wide acceptance of the 'Obama care' law providing many Americans with their first-ever affordable health insurance.

In June 2022, with several conservative judges who were already on record as devoted to striking down abortion access on the Supreme Court of the United States, thanks to President Trump's actions in his first term, both *Roe* and *Planned Parenthood* were reversed. One could see the triumphalist anti-choice philosophy in the Court's reasoning:

'Before this Court, petitioners [the anti-choice group] defend the Act [the Mississipi statute that prohibited abortions past the 15th week of pregnancy] on the grounds that *Roe* and *Casey* were wrongly decided and that the Act is constitutional because it satisfies rational-basis review.

> *Held:* The Constitution does not confer a right to abortion; *Roe* and *Casey* (*Planned Parenthood v Casey*) are overruled; and the authority to regulate abortion is returned to the people and their elected representatives.
>
> When the Supreme Court of the United States says that something is 'Held', that is final. There is no appeal from the US Supreme Court to any other body, national or transnational. There is no appeal to bodies such as the Inter-American Court of Human Rights because the United States has not become a party to any of the major international courts.

It further needs to be said that in other countries, there is a constitutional court, a separate entity with a separate jurisdiction; but the US Supreme Court is supreme in every area of law.

The talk about 'the people and their elected representatives' in the quote above seems to empower ordinary people. But, especially in the US south, where African-American voters have long been restricted in their voting behaviour due both to the notorious gerrymandering of electoral districts and to overly onerous requirements about voter identificatio, even literacy (which is not demanded in most other countries, with countries in the global South often having easily recognized logos that voters can check, and/or colours), the American people being actually empowered by the Supreme Court are the largely white and mainly evangelical Republican politicians[4] in state legislatures.

There is little doubt that if most state legislatures in 2022 had been under firm Democratic control the Supreme court would not have invoked voting for legislatures with the same pretend-democratic fervour. For this chapter's purposes, it is worth knowing that these right-wing judges and their allies in the MAGA-controlled state legislatures are the same people who have spoken up for parental control of all matters concerning schooling. The state legislatures in Republican states have gone so far as to impose requirements that parents of trans youth be informed of their child's decision to change their pronouns and/or names.[5] Hence, the rather dire situation of trans youth in much of the United States is closely linked to the legal situation of women, deprived of the abortion rights that people thought had been permanently won in 1973.

The talk of democracy is thus a double-edged sword, in a country with a long and painful history of *de facto* discrimination against Black and poor voters that survived the granting of *de jure* equality rights to African-Americans. But it is important to note as well that women's right to choose was taken away not by invoking public morals (as would have been the case a century earlier) but rather by a court that sought to wrap its anti-choice message in the language of 'the people' and state-level democracy. The result has been a confusing situation where women in some states not only have the right to get an abortion but doctors are able to send abortion pills by mail to women in 'red' (conservative) states, through the operation of what are known as 'shield'

4 Not all politicians claiming allegiance to evangelical principles and theology are sincere evangelicals, any more than politicians who claim to be pro-choice are necessarily pro-feminist. Abortion has become a political football, and not only in the United States. Donald Trump, notoriously, seems personally more libertarian than evangelical. And yet he constantly seeks and mostly obtains the 'evangelical vote', despite conducting himself in his family and sexual life in ways that defy evangelical morality.

5 Privacy law is today seen as a safeguard against data collection by major tech companies and state security agencies, but that is a recent development. In the United States, privacy in the contemporary, anti-surveillance sense has only existed in law since the federal Privacy Act of 1974.

laws, laws protecting medical practitioners and women who take advantage of the new, non-surgical, purely pharmaceutical methods for procuring an abortion.

Be that as it may, the Supreme Court's 2022 decision shifted the scale of the political battle (as geographers would say). States that had generally voted Democrat by and large preserved the right to abortion, even, as a resisting response to the 2022 decision, sometimes enshrining it in the state constitution. But in the vast swaths of the nation where state legislatures are largely Republican, and in many cases have had representatives elected specifically on an anti-choice platform, there is no recourse in either mass action or in law against the Supreme Court's 'Held'. Abortion pills might continue to be sent in the mail, but states like Texas have passed laws that reward ordinary citizens who bring abortions to the attention of the authorities. On May 27, the Daily podcast, run by the New York Times, documented a case of a boyfriend or partner denouncing his girlfriend to the authorities, after finding out that the girlfriend had obtained an abortion pill through the post. The Texas statute, therefore, empowers individual men, not only police officers, to denounce women for breaking the draconian state abortion law.

Outside of the United States, the battles about abortion rights have taken a different form. In Argentina, for example, there was a huge popular movement around 2019–2020, marked by the green kerchiefs worn by women protesters, that led the government (a government controlled by the reasonably progressive Peronista party) to legalize abortion, in 2020. There is no doubt that massive street level protests leading up to the legislative change were far more important in that context than any constitutional or other type of legal battle.

One interesting feature of some civil-law jurisdictions is that the Criminal Code proclaims women's sexual autonomy as a distinct right. That is a different theoretical basis for abortion rights than the purely individualistic 'privacy' of US laws. In Spain, for instance, rape and sexual assault are criminalized as offences not against public morals or public order (as indecency and obscenity still are in most common-law jurisdictions) but rather offences against women's sexual autonomy. There is no legal control on women's right to abortion in the first fourteen weeks of pregnancy, and provision is made for abortions until up to 22 weeks in particular health-related cases.

'Sexual autonomy', interestingly, is a major principle in Spanish criminal law. It seems to address gender violence specifically. Since it is gendered, it differs significantly from the American 'right to privacy', which remains rather abstract and disembodied unless empirically connected to particular situations. The protection of sexual autonomy is also a phrase that acknowledges that sexual activity is something women might positively want, as opposed to the American notion of 'privacy', which simply says the state needs to butt out, and is quite compatible with sex negativity.

French law, on its part, has proclaimed a woman's right to choose as a constitutional right since 1975. And as was the case in Argentina, the campaign in France was not mainly in courts, but rather on the streets. In France, major feminist intellectuals such as Simone de Beauvoir signed an open letter declaring that they too had had abortions (which would have been illegal, before 1975).

Elsewhere, some Christian denominations have waged major campaigns to ban or restrict abortion rights. The Catholic church, in particular, has fought against legalizing abortion all through Latin America – perhaps in a vain attempt to retain their market share in the face of successful Protestant missionary efforts, some of them funded by US-based churches.

Ireland is the best example of a longstanding prohibition on abortion justified by reference to Catholic theology, which has long tried to divide 'natural' from 'unnatural' (non-reproductive) sexuality. Nevertheless, with the sharp decline in prestige of the Catholic church over the past twenty years (with many priests being charged with child abuse either in courts of law or in the court of public opinion), the political scene changed significantly. As a result, in 2018 the abortion law was changed to allow for abortions on demand up to twelve weeks of pregnancy – whereas in earlier decades Irish women and girls with unwanted pregnancies had to get themselves to England, where some clinics specialized in Irish clients. (Flights are not necessary, since there was and still is ferry service between Ireland and England.)

Throughout all of these social protests and legislative changes, Canada remains an almost unique jurisdiction in that there is no criminal law on abortion at all. The story of the decriminalization of abortion in Canada is quite contingent; it says nothing about any national values or national consciousness. The facts are that in January of 1988, the Supreme Court of Canada struck down the then prevailing law as unconstitutional, namely in that it breached the relatively new Charter of Rights and Freedoms. After many legislative manouvres, both major parties (Liberals and Conservatives) abandoned the seemingly fruitless task of trying to pass a new abortion law that would garner sufficient votes in Parliament.

What is very noticeable in relation to the wider field of health law is that in almost every country where some abortions are legal, generally as exceptions to an otherwise blanket criminal prohibition, there is usually a rather arbitrary temporal cut-off point. Sometimes that is justified through the medical or pseudo-medical notion of 'fetal viability'. And yet, since medical advances are constantly redefining the timing of 'viability', it would seem pointless to try to set out in a statute a point after which abortions are rendered illegal or at least in need of a special exemption.

After the temporal point set out in the criminal code, in most jurisdictions, pregnant women have to seek special permission to have what is otherwise a medical procedure like so many others.[6] Time limits such as those that exist in Spain, Ireland, and the many states of the United States in which abortion remains legal, are not generally applied to other medical procedures such as heart transplants or lung transplants.

One could read the time limits (which are always subject to exceptions and to change over time, as 'fetal viability' changes) as a pragmatic 'compromise' between political ideologies. Perhaps that is the empirical origin of the otherwise rather arbitrary time limits, which differ widely across jurisdictions. But one can also note that no medical procedure that is typically masculine is subject to any time limits, and/or to the availability of doctors willing and able to perform the procedure. The location of abortion law in the criminal code of any country is problematic from a feminist 'reproductive rights' perspective.

Why Pick On Trans Kids?

Let us now shift to the current campaigns against trans people, especially trans children and youth, perhaps the other key current arena on which the governance of bodies through coercive law is being fought out now.

Very few people choose to change their gender, compared to the millions of women facing unwanted pregnancies every year in every country in the world. This is understandable: gender represents a major part of one's personal identity, and is usually well established psychologically and physically even before puberty. So why is there such a moral panic? The moral panic is disguised as a fear that 'fake' women might enter women's bathrooms and/or enjoy an unfair advantage in women's sports (as seen recently in the case of the University of Pennsylvania losing millions in federal funding because of the presence of a single trans woman athlete in the varsity swim team). Moral panics often express deep-seated fears about a phenomenon that is not significant numerically but poses a threat to the prevalent ideology, and that seems to be the case here, given the tiny numbers of trans youth.

In general, moral panics occur when a single issue – a perceived single issue, that is – is actually not single at all, but is rather the vector sum of a variety of diverse major anxieties and cultural worries. Illicit drugs, for example, are stigmatized for a whole host of reasons. Drugs can arguably be said to have constituted a moral panic in many countries at different times – and

6 The widespread availability of 'abortion pills' even in those states in the United States that ban relevant operations (since pills can be sent through the mail, including from Mexico, a regular source of cheaper medications for Americans), may be making some of the regulations aimed at conventional surgeries irrelevant. The availability of pills to bring on a period in US states that otherwise ban abortions, often almost all abortions, is reminscent of the late nineteenth century, when doctors and self-made businessmen openly advertised 'remedies' in newspaper advertisements for products meant to 'bring on your period' or 'make women regular'.

that is not merely because illicit drugs may contain fentanyl or be otherwise bad for one's health.

When child abductions constitute a moral panic, which happens every so often in many countries, that fear too is grounded in a whole host of reasons. People may intellectually know, through reading or education, that the home is the most likely space for child abuse: but that does not mean that the fear of 'stranger danger' is absent or is addressed by the production of statistics that would tend to cast doubts on the probability of the fear. Social media undoubtedly contributes to the dissemination of the kinds of fears that fuel moral panics. There are well established urban legends, for instance, that purport to fuel American people's fears of crossing into Mexico by raising the spectre of involuntary organ donation. (The urban legend in question often starts with 'I woke up in a bathtub full of ice…') One can easily see why the Mexican and not the Canadian border would be regarded with this extreme suspicion, not just by MAGA Americans but to other more mainstream citizens as well.

The case of trans youth likely became a moral panic – not only in Republican-dominated parts of the United States but elsewhere, such as in the Canadian province of Alberta, and in many South American countries – because it triggered and amplified several existing social anxieties.[7] Public perceptions about the 'decline of the nuclear family' (mentioned in the previous chapter in a different context) united with fears about gender being far too unstable in this age of gender-bending and tales about drag queens reading children's books to kids in public libraries.

On top of that, or perhaps underlying the other anxieties, is the ever-present fear that many parents have about potentially losing authority either to the state's education system or to the welfare state – full of Dickensian children's homes (as seen in TV shows and other instances of popular culture) and evil foster parents. Demonizing state care has the effect of making 'the family' seem safer, whether that is true in individual cases or not.

My argument here is not that fears about gendered dangers and child disappearances are unjustified. It is merely that there must be a reason why many anti-trans policies target public schools in particular, rather than targeting either overly liberal parents or overly conservative ones. In many countries, 'the state' is visible in family life mainly in the form of public schools. Many of the currently favoured anti-trans laws and policies insist that parents of children who choose to change their gender and/or their name be informed about 'their' child's choice. This requirement can and likely is designed to put those children and youth at risk. Many youth and an unknown number of children do not feel comfortable discussing their gender and sexual and gender

7 For more on moral panics see Mariana Valverde, *The Age of Light, Soap and Water: Moral Reform in English Canada 1880s–1920s* (Toronto, McClelland and Stewart 1991; University of Toronto Press, second edition 2010), Chapters 2 and 3.

anxieties and desires with their parents. For many youth and children, parental violence is a far greater risk than the rather fantastical spectre of LGBTQ teachers 'grooming' kids and persuading them to be gay in their classes.

In the 1970s and 1980s there were major moral panics – in the United States led by orange-juice queen and fervent evangelical Anita Bryant – about 'pedophiles' in positions of authority. Gay and lesbian teachers were then the major enemy, the key threat to what was often called 'the safety of the family' (once again one has to consider the persistent weight of the 'haven in a heartless world' myth that grounds planning law rules in common-law countries as well as anti-trans policies).

However, the LGBTQ movement managed to accomplish what the pro-choice on abortion movement never managed to obtain, which was a considerable measure of respectability. This was partly through the legal availability of same-sex marriage in many jurisdictions, a legal change whose cultural consequences have yet to be thoroughly mapped.

In the new world of cosmopolitan diversity, especially urban diversity, adult gays and lesbians can no longer be easily cast as villains poisoning 'our' kids' minds. If those previously shunned gays and lesbians chose to get married and/or had children who looked and acted quite 'normal', most of the wind is taken out of the sails of plain old homophobia. Such couples even buy houses together, as the literature on 'gay gentrification' shows. And one can ask: what is a greater signifier of moral worthiness in North America than home ownership? (See previous chapter for more on this).

The rise of what I have called the 'respectable same-sex couple'[8] is in my view closely connected to the changed emphasis on policing the names and pronouns of kids and youth rather than going after adult gays and lesbians. Adult gays and lesbians are now visible almost everywhere, even in police forces and in armies. Targeting them would require a huge effort, and many within the state apparatus would now be unwilling to engage in this witch-hunt. But trans youth? How many of them do we personally know? I happen to know quite a few, because many university students, as they build their adult selves, decide that they were always non-binary or the 'opposite' gender from that assigned at birth. (More could be said about the heterosexist myths perpetrated by the phrase 'opposite-sex', but we will leave that for readers to ponder).

And I do personally know many university students, hence my biased sample. But in the larger society the situation is different. In the larger society, gender fears may be pervasive, but they don't necessarily coalesce in the kind of single threatening image that sparks moral panics. The non-binary or trans

8 Mariana Valverde, 'A New Entity in the History of Sexuality: The Respectable Same-Sex Couple' *Feminist Studies* vol. 31 no. 2 (2006), 155–162. For a more recent critique of the attacks on queer and trans lives, see Judith Butler, *Who's Afraid of Gender?* (Toronto, Alfred Knopf, 2024).

youth may be more of a media image than a picture of real people we personally know.

In the broader society, trans people and especially trans youth are almost invisible, with a few notable and corageous exceptions. They thus make easier targets. They can be turned into the witches that are pursued in witchhunts, scapegoats for a whole range of perceived familial and socio-cultural ills.

In Canada, where gays and lesbians are encouraged to join the national military, Alberta's new law attacking the identity autonomy of LGBTQ and especially trans kids is one of the many contemporary examples of what theorist Judith Butler has dubbed a gender panic. She analyzes this panic in her recent book 'Who's Afraid of Gender?' (2024) She (or rather 'they') mentions travelling to Brazil and Argentina and witnessing an all-out attack on the very queer theory that she/they are famous for, all in the name of the 'traditional' family and what in the United States is called 'parental control'. In Latin America especially the leadership of the Catholic church has been particularly active in waging a culture war against what is often called 'the ideology of gender'. (As if the patriarchal myth of the father-knows-best nuclear family was not ideological.)

The racist roots of parental control, furthermore, are clear to anyone who looks into the history of 'parents' choice' in schooling. In the United States, a backlash against teachers (and teachers' unions) was very much part of the backlash against integrated classrooms. The US Supreme Court's decision in 2022 that overturned *Roe* and *Planned Parenthood* was said to be justified by recourse to 'the people' and their elected representatives. So too, any statement that makes the questionable assumption that elections to the state legislature are fair and non-discriminatory need fact-checking, especially in southern states. So too, the attack on trans people and especially youth was justified by referring to 'parental control'. As if only parents were citizens. And as if all citizens were parents.

Parental control is thus the family-scale version of the myth of 'the people' and their elected representatives that the US Supreme Court (the most powerful non-elected body in the land, one must recall) mobilized. That the US Supreme Court would justify its anti-choice decision by reference to 'the people' and their elected representatives was a huge contradiction, not noted by many commentators.

This contradiction was seen in the discussion of abortion rights, where parental control was not in play, as such, but old-fashioned patriarchy was. If democracy in the United States is more theoretical and abstract than practically real, as numerous critics have argued, perhaps parental control too is a bit of a myth – for the same reasons.

These days, most youth pay far more attention to their phones than to their parents' advice. (I say this as the parent of two young people.) And that is not just in the United States. It's everywhere that data plans for one's phone or wifi access are available.

This sheds light on the quest of the premier of conservative politicians raising fears about trans people and insisting on total parental control of young people and their bodies. Whether the conservative quest to limit women's autonomy and impose what is in the age of social media the fiction of 'parental control' will succeed or fail is not clear. Much depends on what happens in the next decade or so.

Conclusions

The scale of the body turns out not to be, in the real world of politics and fights about competing rights, the scale of *all* human bodies. Bodies are never generic. They are raced, gendered, of a certain age, and are either disabled or not. Male white bodies seem to have been largely exempt from regulation, in imperial ventures and also closer to home. Women's bodies do come under the gaze of the state even today, in the way that choice on abortion is either given (grudgingly, with time limits) or withheld, through the criminalization of abortion. Partial decriminalization is still criminalization – as gays and lesbians told that sexual conduct taking place in private spaces and between two and no more than two consenting adults would be legalized, as an exception to the overall and continuing ban on homosexuality.[9]

As long as women but not men need to seek permission – even when reproductive choice is left 'between a woman and her doctor' – for a medical procedure, whereas no masculine medical procedure is subject to any such criminal-law controls, women are not free.

The expansive concept of 'reproductive freedom' is the larger umbrella within which abortion rights huddle. The term was devised back in the 1970s to cover such notorious absences of women's autonomy as China's once-strict one-child policy. 'Reproductive freedom' also covers such denials of autonomy and freedom as the compulsory and/or secret sterilization of Indigenous women and women of colour that has existed in different countries at different times.

Thus, abortion rights are only the most visible of the many struggles for reproductive freedom that women have faced at different times. And many feminists, including the present writer, believe that until abortion is fully taken out of the criminal code, women's freedom will be limited in a specifically

9 The partial legalization was usually hailed as a great liberatory move – for instance by former Prime Minister of Canada Pierre Trudeau, who famously introduced his 1969 criminal code reforms (legalizing contraception and partially decriminalizing homosexuality and abortion) with the ringing and oft-quoted phrase 'the state has no place in the bedrooms of the nation'. Policing actions in Canada over the ten or fifteen years following Pierre Trudeau's governments would cast doubt on Trudeau's grandiose statement.

gendered way. Having to seek permission for any medical procedure, even a so-called 'late' abortion, is NOT being free to choose.

Unfortunately, solidarity between women who were rewarded by the state for having either many or just one child and those women who seek and need abortion rights has often been swept under the rug and out of public view. But reproductive freedom (which goes well with gender identity autonomy for all, including youth) is the larger goal of the feminist health movement. And to repeat, abortion simply does not belong in the criminal code – any more than prostate cancer treatment.

At the level not of the individual body but of 'the family', it seems that today's anxieties about the perceived decline of 'the family' (meaning the two-parent heterosexual father-knows-best nuclear family) and the fears regarding the current instability or fluidity of gender categories once thought to be fixed by nature can converge to create any number of moral panics, abortion being only one of many targets. A key act of self-affirmation and autonomy that law in many US states and at least one Canadian province seeks to ban or control is a young person's decision to change their name and/or their gender to what seems more 'natural' to them.

Numbers are important for political purposes. That is likely why heterosexual white women seeking reproductive freedom, who are often active in mainstream political parties, have been largely successful. They have had more power, including as judges and lawyers, than most other women (poor and Indigenous women in particular). And lesbian as well as gay male couples, if leading respectable lives that include home ownership, and engaged in such classic American behaviour as lawn care, turned out to be less of a threat, especially when allowed to marry, than was anticipated in the 1970s and 1980s.

It turned out, contrary to the fears about 'pedophiles' being stoked in many places, that lesbian couples and gay male couples could be accommodated within structures meant for 'families' without too much disturbance. It was just a matter of adding a new demographic to the established pattern of family life. The mortgage market was certainly happy to take in gay and lesbian couples seeking to buy a home.

Trans kids and youth, by contrast, are far less numerous, so the average person is not likely to know many. In addition there is a certain anxiety about gender that many people, including middle-aged adults, have. Trans youth, who wittingly or not are challenging one of the key cultural binaries of almost every culture (male/female) are hence more easily turned into a scapegoat for everything that seems to have gone wrong in contemporary societies. Just about every straight person, at least in cities, knows a gay or lesbian co-worker, boss, neighbour, fellow dog-owner, and so on. But trans kids and trans youth are more easily targeted, perhaps precisely because during most of the rise of LGBTQ rights in the 1970s and 1980s they seemed absent. Trans kids and youth are thus a relatively new threat.

But in the end, it is true that queer theory, and especially queer geography as developed by queer theorists and empirical researchers[10] does challenge gender as such – gender as a or even THE fundamental structure of society.

As long as the first question asked of new parents is 'is it a boy or a girl?', as if the baby cared one way or the other, gender and gender identity will continue to be a source of anxiety and fear for many people. In past decades similar anxieties attached to Black bodies and/or pregnant women's bodies. Those racial and gendered anxieties have by no means disappeared; but in many places people have learned to live with racial and gender difference. The fact that women are now filling law schools and medical schools without too much of a backlash is telling here.[11]

The right-wing answer to any and all questions about gender and identity, questions that are genuinely troubling many families, is 'parental control'. Parental control may be in relation to trans kids and youth what states' rights was to African-Americans.

Young people may need their autonomy more than adults, who can choose their friends with relative freedom. Sexual and gender autonomy for youth may sometimes set them against 'parental control', especially in right-wing jurisdictions. And yet we know without explanations being necessary that not all parents are created equal. Trans-positive parents and grandparents are not particularly empowered by legislation that furthers what is always called 'parental control'.

The disempowering of some parents over others is exactly what right-wing anti-woke cultural and political trends do not take into account. In the United States, invoking 'the people' who elect state legislatures is not always a sign of effective democracy (as seen in the Supreme Court's decision striking

10 See the geography journal *Gender, Space and Place* for numerous examples of contemporary queer geography, much of it paying close attention to legal rules.

11 One could argue that respectable gays and lesbians have become visible just as being queer was no longer the dreadful secret it was for decades. Critical queer literature on 'homonationalism' is especially relevant on this point. The state of Israel, for example, has long been accused of 'pink washing' as it has been foregrounding the legally equal status of gays and lesbians in Israel (implicitly or explicitly contrasted with the assumed homophobia of majority-Muslim countries). Many geographers are today writing about 'homonationalism'.

down abortion rights). Such invocations can just as well be a not very thinly disguised return to the Civil War southern cry of 'states' rights'.[12][13]

In the United States, white supremacy and anti-Black racism are never far from the surface. Other issues (urban poverty, for instance, and of course public schooling) are often shaped, quietly or not, by the long national history of anti-Black racism and its forms of power/knowledge.

While other countries may not encourage 'home schooling' in the same way as is done in the United States, rising numbers of children in private schools and especially the often lavish public funding of semi-private and religious (Christian) schools may well indicate a similar anti-integration and anti-state mentality.

Sexual and gender autonomy may look like a distant goal, but as Martin Luther King might have said, one has to be facing in the right direction to even get a small start.

12 For biographical reasons I completed grade eight in the United States, Charlottesville, Virginia to be precise. There, my history teacher (white of course; all the teachers of every subject except Physical Education were white) insisted time and again that the Civil War – still an almost living memory in that town, home to Thomas Jefferson and his many slaves – was not about slavery. It was rather about 'states' rights'. I do not recall whether our textbook followed that line or not – I suspect not, or the teacher would not have had to make such a point of insisting in class that the Civil War was NOT about slavery. But the textbook might have been forcibly imposed on the school, as desegregation had been a few years earlier.

13 See the detailed historically grounded analysis of the Trump administration's efforts to defund or even abolish the federal Department of Education: Diane Ravitch, 'Selling Out Our Public Schools' *New York Review of Books* March 13, 2025, pp. 32–35.

Conclusion

It was mainly in the 1980s that legal geography began to develop as a subfield of both legal studies and geography (especially urban geography)[1]. At its inception, the attention of scholars (often in collaboration with activists) was directed mainly at new measures that sought to replace old-style vagrancy statutes. Vagrancy and similar status offences were falling to constitutional challenges in many places, which meant, for legislators at various levels, especially the local level, that new legal means had to be devised to promote or maintain urban order.

This was achieved, or at least encouraged, largely through measures that sought to exercise control over 'the usual suspects'. The targeting of the traditional 'disorderly people' would now be done not through criminal statutes targeting specific statuses, but rather through what US municipal law calls 'time, place and manner' rules.

The exploration of the legal measures that usually replaced vagrancy statutes when those were declared unconstitutional by many courts and some legislatures focused initially on general-application by-laws and ordinances (the sort of rules discussed in Chapters 3 and 4).

A whole host of studies of measures were devised, and by and large these were implicitly or explicitly based on 'broken-windows' criminology.[2] Broken windows and 'zero tolerance' policing were in great vogue in the 1980s and 1990s. They were based on the assumption or the theory that minor disorders and marginal disorderly people who are committing no crimes need control and possibly punishment because allowing them free rein will

1 An early anthology that sought to represent 'the field' was Nicholas Blomley, David Delaney and Richard Ford, eds., *The Legal Geographies Reader: Law, Power and Space* (Oxford, Wiley-Blackwell, 2001). A later anthology with some of the same authors sought to include the temporalities that are enshrined in law, as well as spaces: Irus Braverman, Nicholas Blomley, David Delaney and Sandy Kedar, *The Expanding Spaces of Law* (Stanford California, Stanford University Press 2017).

2 For a detailed critique, on its own empiricist terms, of broken-windows criminology, see Bernard Harcourt, *The Illusion of Order: The False Promise of Broken Windows Policing* (Cambridge MA, Harvard University Press, 2001).

DOI: 10.4324/9781003612551-8

inevitably lead to crime and major disorders. Broken windows criminology became so widely accepted that it almost turned into 'common sense', despite the fact that many academic criminologists were highly critical of it. Broken-windows assumptions were generally used to sustain the cultural prejudices of the dominant groups in urban environments. The original 1982 'broken windows' article, published in the US magazine *The Atlantic*, was illustrated with pencil drawings of women soliciting men for paid sex, men clearly meant to look alcoholic lying on sidewalks, and other traditional symbols of urban disorder. The sort of urban-order measures enabled by broken-windows discourse were critically analyzed by geographers, critical urbanists and some legal scholars. But since police departments and many lay community groups had swallowed the broken-windows kool-aid, the critiques, often published in scholarly venues, did not significantly shift public opinion. It was only in the twenty-first century that 'common sense' began to grapple with the fraying of the social safety net under neoliberalism, and began to call for more social services and more youth programs, instead of trying to find ways to punish and control the 'disorderly'.

Municipalities and other local governments often developed not just rules of general application but, as seen in chapter 4 especially, rules seeking to govern the poor and those deemed disorderly through 'time, space and manner' restrictions. (The 'time, space and manner' powers of municipalities have been more extensive than liberal political thought has assumed; in the United States, these powers are known as 'the police power of the state', which despite its name is largely municipal.)

These rules often applied only to specific sites (especially tourist- and professional sports-oriented 'premium' or privileged spaces, often on waterfronts or other spaces considered especially desirable). That is the subject of Chapter 4. Often, however, the rules were general, that is, they applied formally throughout the municipal territory or space of local government, but were enforced only selectively – for example in major raids just before major sports events (the Olympics or the World Cup). It is important to know that municipalities rarely employ the number of municipal inspectors that would be necessary for consistent city-wide enforcement; municipal inspectors are generally far fewer in number than police officers, who often have the power to enforce local rules but who pride themselves on 'going after criminals' (despite criminological research showing that crime fighting takes up a small portion of police officer time).

Within these type of urban-order campaign, the rules that were alread in place governing competing users of parks, sidewalks and other public spaces took pride of place. Often, new statutes and by-laws/ordinances were devised: in Ontario, where I live, the provincial government passed the 'Safe Streets Act' in 2001, once it was clear that municipalities lacked the legal power to ban activities such as begging and squeeging.

It was shown fairly quickly, through successful litigation and in scholarly analyses, that rules such as 'it is forbidden to set up a tent to camp overnight in a public park' were discriminatory in effects, if not on their face. Human rights law by the twenty-first century had become used to the phrases 'systemic effects' and 'systemic discrimination'. This was useful, since many of the urban-order rules inspired by broken-windows criminology were on their face common-sense rules governing public spaces, such as sidewalks, or parks. It was only when evidence about the unequal effects of discriminatory enforcement was put forward that courts struck down some of these new rules as unconstitutional. (The 'discovery' of police racial profiling helped many observers including local politicians to appreciate systemic effects.) In the global North as well as the South, unhoused people and very poor people are far more likely to experience a need to set up tents in public parks, much more than those who were living in 'normal' family households in 'normal' homes (Chapter 5 targets the bourgeois patriarchal breadwinner family ideology that is embedded in many zoning and planning regimes).

The focus often changed away from rules of general application to specific (and even site-specific) rules that inscribed existing social hierarchies literally on the ground. In the UK, ASBOs (Anti-Social Behaviour Orders) were devised and applied in site-specific ways, but they also named specific people as threats to community order – which would have been deemed unconstitutional in many other countries.

Critical legal geography and critical urban studies analyzed these new-ish rules. Much of this literature consisted of case studies. Case studies were done of such spaces as public squares that had been partially or wholly privatized, or that were created anew, usually in 'deals' between the city planning officials and developers. Thus, attention was drawn to the relatively new category of POPS, privately owned public spaces. Once upon a time it was clear to the idle passerby which spaces were public and which were private (businesses, homes). But around the turn of the twenty-first century, walking through a city stopped being a method for personally documenting public vs. private spaces, public property vs. private property. Most of the new-ish POPS look public, but are in fact the private property of someone or some corporation (usually, a developer who in exchange for building the little park got extra height on their tower).

Such analyses showed that urban space, far from being the coherent mini-state that had long been envisaged (especially by lawyers) was often very fragmented by and in law.[3] This is documented in chapter 4 in particular, but the theme of the city's lack of legal legibility runs through the book. It turned out, when investigated, usually by a lawyer or an academic, that apparently public

3 For the often neglected active role of downtown Business Improvement Areas or Districts see articles by Kevin Walby and Randy Lippert.

spaces were actually under the control of a private authority. That means that accountability in policing and enforcement is generally very difficult, if not impossible. Private owners in common-law jurisdictions generally use 'trespass to property' statutes or even trespass as a tort, with privately hired and paid private security being usually the operative enforcement agency.

A notable case along these lines were the large protests arising from the 'Occupy Wall Street' movement in the wake of the 2008 global financial crisis. It turned out that the space, open to the public and looking 'public' that was chosen as the main site of the protests, Zucotti park, was actually privately owned. That caused confusion and even chaos. Similar situations developed in other cities: in Vancouver, for example, Occupy protesters moved from one space to another owned by a government entity (the provincial Art Gallery), and in so doing the question of who needed to make a choice to let them stay or boot them out fell to a very different authority.

Despite the apparent legal line separating public (government) from private property, the realities of urban space are far more complicated than the public vs. private binary would suggest.

For one thing, the private owners of urban spaces that look as if they're public parks have often had recourse to private security agents, rather than the public police, to enforce their claims. That makes sense, since what they mainly want is to displace the 'disorderly' people and have them moved elsewhere, even just a block away. Private security guards do not arrest people or charge them with offences: they merely 'move them along'. The logic of private security is thus different from the logic of police who are enforcing the criminal law and the large variety of sub-state laws, such as traffic rules. Thus, whether a space that is open to the public at large is privately owned or is a municipal park makes a huge difference in regard to the tactics used to impose or recreate 'order'.

Business Improvement Districts or 'Improvement Areas' (or other euphemisms, such as British 'regeneration districts') can be an important component of this relatively new assemblage. Infrastructure is now usually delivered through what are known as 'public-private partnerships'. But the new security assemblages are similar. They are marked by a shifting and unpredictable relation between the public police and other bodies of official-looking people, almost always wearing hi-viz vests. These can be park personnel, transit workers, security guards, or other workers, depending on the jurisdiction involved. Automation (such as electronic transit cards replacing bus and tram inspectors and ticket-takers) often threatens their jobs, and privatization can also, even when not promoted by governments, affect their fate: for example, many people now call an Uber instead of taking public transit. The 1960s and 1970s may have been the golden age of uniformed personnel, people who besides doing the job for which they were hired played a quiet or implicit safety and security function. Nowadays, the 'eyes on the street' that Jane Jacobs and others thought was the true key to citizen safety are far less numerous. That decline of various uniformed personnel, linked to both automation and the decline of the welfare state, may be very relevant to the current moral panics about 'unsafe streets', unsafe public transit and unsafe public parks.

Criminological studies of particular campaigns designed to 'clear out' certain problem spaces, always under the banner of 'public safety' (parks, markets, train stations, central bus stations and airports) greatly contributed to our understanding of how law perpetuates existing inequality and how it often amplifies those inequalities. Criminologists, however, often failed to note the difference that separates private property owners from public authorities in enforcement logics. The no longer current term 'social control' had the effect of hiding from view the striking differences between the logic of criminal law enforcement and the logic of private security.

More recently geographers, long absorbed in their collective contemplation of space, began to pay attention to time, to different temporalities embedded in different legal tools, and the rules that govern people differentially though temporal markers. Eminent legal anthropologists, represented by journals such as the *Journal of Legal Pluralism and Unofficial Law*, began to pay as much attention to temporality as to space and place.[4] The relatively new focus on temporality, which for many scholars came well after governance through and of space had come into focus, is reflected in many of the specific rules devised to govern urban legal islands such as those explored in Chapter 4. Often, the rules that govern particular spaces divide day from night in a sharp manner, and there are often also rules, enshrined in antique municipal by-laws, that refer to 'dawn' or 'dusk', despite the inherent vagueness of those terms.[5]

Some geographers, especially writing from queer and/or feminist perspectives, have noticed that in addition to the scales that international law documents (transnational, state-wide, local) there is also a scale of 'the body'. This is the scale that from the outset distinguishes bodies by gender, race, age,

4 One source in which established European anthropologists engaged with temporal questions, some for the first time, was Franz von Benda Beckmann, Kebeet von Benda Beckmann and Anne Griffiths, eds., *Spatializing Law: An Anthropological Geography of Law in Society* (London, Ashgate, 2009). Concrete studies of particular legal temporalities are fascinating. See S. Beynon-Jones and E. Grabham, eds, *Law and Time* (London, Routledge, 2018). Emily Grabham, a British legal scholar of temporality, has produced detailed studies of various temporalities created by and for law, such as the different times that employment law and other type of laws set for maternity leave.

5 One example is a seldom-enforced Toronto by-law that applies to ice-cream trucks. Such trucks are prohibited from playing the familiar ice-cream truck music after 'dusk'. I know this because a former student's father had an ice-cream truck licence. The then student told me that a zealous municipal inspector attempted to fine him, a Greek immigrant, for playing the music well into the evening. This happened to be on a day when a major power outage in August meant that people were out on the street and seeking ice-cream, their privately owned refrigerators no longer operating.

disability, and other factors. Today's political battles about abortion rights for women and trans rights especially for kids and youth have a very concrete, material dimension that is determined by the perceived threats that particular bodies are seen to pose to the social order. The current US Republican panic about 'fake women' utilizing trans trans accommodation measures to 'take over' women's public bathrooms and women's sports is but the latest campaign. This and previous campaigns against 'gender' highlight the growing distance between the documented risk that certain people pose to others and the perceived threat. The Olympics have long engaged in systemically sexist gender testing of women athletes, paying no attention to some men's inordinate height or other features that make them excel in sports. But that kind of gender-testing is widely tolerated, under the banner of protecting the 'integrity' of women's sports, which is seen as threatened by the very occasional trans (M to F) person who plays as a woman. The politics of the body are particularly visible in Olympic and professional sports. (One example being the non-binary football player on the Canadian women's soccer team, who only uses one name, Quinn.)

In the United States, currently, the presence of a single trans woman in a university swim team is seen as grounds for withdrawing federal funding from the whole university.[6]

The scale of the body, which affects all of us, deemed normal or not, reminds us that law is not simply a set of abstract principles contained in legal treatises. Law is governance (of a special kind) and governance is an everyday affair. As the late great French thinker Michel Foucault put it, we all both govern and are governed, all the time.

What some sociologists like to call 'resistance' or 'agency' is in Foucault's vision just another example of governance –bottom up, perhaps, and not as powerful as the top-down governance of established authorities, but governance nevertheless. When Foucault says 'power is everywhere' that is precisely what he means – that is, that there is no categorical difference between governing and resisting. Every effort to govern others, whether successful or not, whether backed by the coercive force of the state or not, is an exercise of power.

Scholarly work in legal geography and adjacent pursuits is all about documenting differences in the way that power-knowledges are deployed. Paying attention to the switch from one type of legal or political rule to another helps us see a great deal about how everyday life takes place.

Scale, a term long used primarily in map-making, is a very useful term in the study of power relations and governance in general. As chapters 3 and 4 explain at some length, 'seeing like a city' is not the same as seeing like

6 This happened in early 2025 to the University of Pennsylvannia swim team, as ample press coverage revealed.

a state but over a smaller area: there are significant qualitative differences between the scale of the nation-state and that of local government, just as there are between the scale of imperialism and colonialism on the one hand and the scale of the nation-state on the other.[7]

Foucault put forward the idea that forms of objectification (meaning how people and activities are turned into objects of problematization, of research and of official or unofficial policy) went with or were often tied to particular forms of subjectification. Subjectification in his language is not about 'agency' – it is about how humans are made into subjects, subjects of the monarch as well as grammatical subjects. Foucault was interested in looking at how different ways of establishing subjectivity work, from being diagnosed as abnormal to being rewarded for being labelled as smart. These tend to go hand in hand with forms of objectification, which might include being counted for census purposes, registering as a student in a university, and so on.

There is is no general theory that can explain the links between objectification and its forms and subjectification and its various forms. The theories that are marketed as 'general' or even 'universal' tend to be very abstract, being detached, on purpose, from everyday situations. That was, in my view, the fatal flaw of Marx's theory: it purported to be a theory of the capitalist economy as such, instead of being a theory of British industrial capitalism in the nineteenth century.

Studies of how subjectivity and objectification have connected or diverged, such as those that Foucault famously produced, have to be site-specific, culture-specific and historically specific.

Currently the main targets or scapegoats for right-wing ideologies seem to be trans youth and pregnant women seeking abortions, as seen in Chapter 6. There is also a backlash against 'equity and diversity' policies in government agencies and n private enterprise. The two campaigns are not unrelated, since racial fears are gendered and sexual fears are racialized (and not only in the United States). A panic about the instability of gender identities that were once thought to be universal and stable bears a striking resemblance to past panics about 'race mixing'. The fears of what US law used to call 'miscegenetion' are more than implicit in the right-wing theories about non-whites or non-Christians 'replacing' white middle-class cultures. That the dominant group (by race and/or gender) should portray itself as a victim rather than as

7 Legal geographers sometimes confuse 'the nation' with 'the state'. Federalism is meant to capture the difference between nations and states. And yet, not all federal nations are multinational, and not all multinational states are federal. India is federal, for example, but the Modi government is busy trying to meld the state with an imagined, romanticized Hindu nation. Concrete analyses of concrete situations are necessary to probe the overlap or otherwise of 'the nation' and 'the state'. Chapter 2 was about the scale of the (modern) state. Many modern states are multinational, including the UK.

the aggressor is a curious phenomenon, but it is not new, having had many historical antecedents.

But what is most urgent? The scale of global climate change? Or the scale of small-group interactions, in the workplace or in the household? In my view there's one thing that Nazi history teaches us: namely, that the main target or scapegoat chosen by a nasty regime can change relatively quickly, with some of the techniques perfected to govern or suppress one subordinate group coming to be applied, often without much thought, to other groups. With the Nazis, first it was the 'feeble-minded' population that was targeted either for sterilization or for genocide, then, communists and their sympathizers, also seen as 'lives not worth living', in the curious Nazi phrase; then Slavic peoples; then homosexuals and Roma people, and finally all Jews, no matter how German or how how respectable. We all know how that movie ended.

And most of us do not want to wait around for the sequel. Feeling that one has to choose among allies or among peoples to support is arguably a symptom of a consumer culture that sees everything as a matter of choosing this or that commodity. The notion of a coalition of groups that remain distinct but support one another puts that consumer-choice model in question. It says that one can have a main 'affinity group' but one can still support others in similar positions.

By way of conclusion: this book as a whole is a plea for what geographers call 'multi-scalar' analyses. There is no good reason why activism, say on urban poverty and homelessness, should not take the 'global' scale of climate change on board, at least some of the time. In fact it is within activist circles that one often finds multi-scalar analyses being taken more or less for granted. In the urban food security movement, for example, connecting nearby farmers to underprivileged neighbourhood markets performs a two-scale or even three-scale move: the global flow of food commodities is connected to the scale of neighbourhood inequality, urban spatial inequality. And all the activities, not only farming, are conducted under the looming shadow of climate change. Multi-scalar analysis sounds like a difficult theoretical move, but it is being done all the time by numerous activist groups.

The choice of specific campaign or project is yours, as they say in the reproductive freedom struggle.

Legal geography provides useful tools for understanding how human life has come to be governed at different scales with different legal and governance tools. But no legal geography and no purely scholarly pursuit can tell anyone what to do or what is the best choice in any particular situation. As Karl Marx said in a different context, social science and legal scholarship cannot write recipes for the kitchens of the future. It will be the cooks of the future that end up writing or amending their own recipes.

Index

Note: Page numbers "n" represent note numbers

Made in the USA
Las Vegas, NV
19 September 2026

7a17bafb-f44e-4c45-b2f1-9e6ab9d768adR01